The Joy of Sox

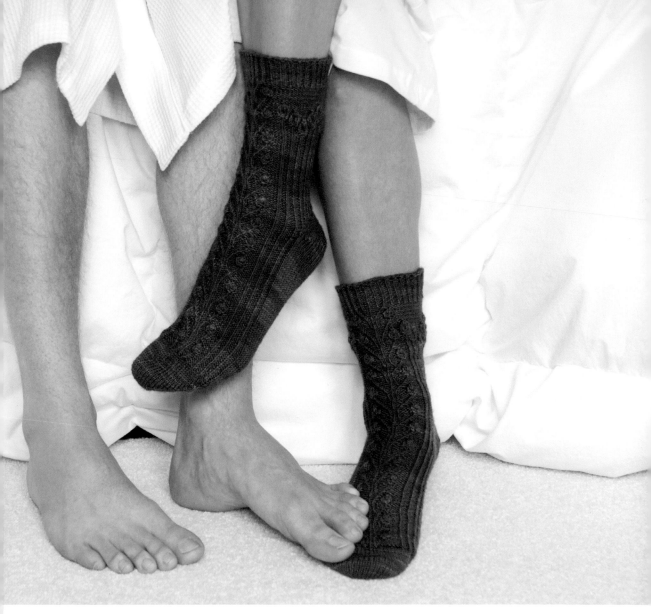

The Joy of Sox

30+ must-knit designs

Linda Kopp

LARK BOOKS

A Division of Sterling Publishing Co., Inc.
New York / London

Editor:
Amanda Carestio

Technical Editor:
Kay J. Hay

Art Director:
Megan Kirby

Production Assistance:
Jeff Hamilton

Illustrator:
Orrin Lundgren

Photography Director:
Dana Irwin

Photographer:
Lynne Harty

Cover Designer:
Celia Naranjo

Library of Congress Cataloging-in-Publication Data

Kopp, Linda, 1960-
  The joy of sox : 30-plus must-knit designs / Linda Kopp. -- 1st ed.
     p. cm.
  Includes index.
  ISBN 978-1-60059-285-0 (hc-plc concealed spiral : alk. paper)
  1. Knitting--Patterns. 2. Socks. I. Title.
  TT825.K694 2009
  746.43'2041--dc22
                                        2009007790

10 9 8 7 6 5 4 3 2 1
First Edition

Published by Lark Books, A Division of Sterling Publishing Co., Inc
387 Park Avenue South, New York, NY 10016

© 2009, Lark Books, a Division of Sterling Publishing Co., Inc.

Distributed in Canada by Sterling Publishing,
c/o Canadian Manda Group, 165 Dufferin Street
Toronto, Ontario, Canada M6K 3H6

Distributed in the United Kingdom by GMC Distribution Services,
Castle Place, 166 High Street, Lewes, East Sussex, England BN7
1XU

Distributed in Australia by Capricorn Link (Australia) Pty Ltd.,
P.O. Box 704, Windsor, NSW 2756 Australia

If you have questions or comments about this book, please contact:
Lark Books, 67 Broadway, Asheville, NC 28801
828-253-0467

Manufactured in China

ISBN 13: 978-1-60059-285-0

For information about custom editions, special sales, premium
and corporate purchases, please contact Sterling Special Sales
Department at 800-805-5489 or specialsales@sterlingpub.com.

Dedicated to all you sock people—you know who you are.
Sock On!

Contents

introduction

Okay, I'll admit it: the pairing of themes (socks and sex) may seem a bit odd at first, but why not? The book needed a title, and I needed a way to share my passion for great sock designs. Knitted socks deserve to be joyful and exciting, in that unbridled, knit-all-night-long kind of way. It's all in good taste, good fun, and—most importantly—great socks.

If you're holding this book in your hands, chances are good that you share my passion for stellar socks. But perhaps, after you've been knitting socks for a while, that once-magical experience began to feel a bit routine: *The Joy of Sox* to the rescue! Start with the Knitty Gritty section for your daily dose of yummy yarn (you know you love it!), interesting ways to use your tools, and detailed instructions for the more involved cast-on and bind-off techniques. Then it's time to move on to the projects, hand-picked for the sock connoisseur. From fantastic cable and lace patterns to killer colorwork, this collection offers the very best in challenging constructions, neat techniques, and tantalizing tips from knitters in the know.

When it comes to socks, it's best to have choices, and with 32 sizzling designs, you're bound to find several you love. The designers selected for this book couldn't help getting inspired by the theme; just take a peek at the ultra-pretty Sweet Nothings (page 160), the worthy-of-a-centerfold Girl's Best Friend Thigh Highs (page 96), and the perfect-for-a-pedicure Peekaboo (page 142).

And this collection of classic socks is 100 percent footsy-approved. From the subtle, yet lovely, Chick Flick (page 112) to the botanical-inspired Make-Up Socks (page 67) to Breakfast in Bed (page 52)—twining, anyone?—I guarantee they'll tempt your needles.

Plus, I've included lots of little extras to tickle your sock-loving fancy: behind-the-scenes tidbits from the sock obsessed, the results of our online sock poll, and knitting adventures from up-and-comers and big-name sock designers alike. Ever wonder how to make the most of hand-painted yarn? See pages 66 and 136 for tips from Shannon Okey and Laura Bryant. Want to read about how an old Suburban changed the course of Kathryn Alexander's knitting career? See page 135. And for a story of woe and triumph, read about Crazy Aunt Purl's first time (complete with scenes on a bus!) on page 88.

So, friends, turn the page, slip into something comfortable, and prepare to put the joy back into making socks.

the knitty gritty

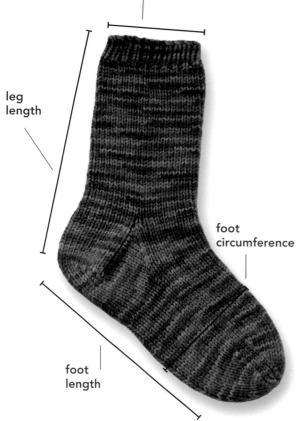

calf circumference

leg length

foot circumference

foot length

Sock Anatomy 101

A simple sock consists of many parts, each of which has a different function and can be worked in a number of ways. Here's a little sock anatomy review: no blushing!

Not all socks emphasize or include all parts. The Peekaboo socks (page 142) don't include toes, and Takeout for Two (page 36) is both toe- and heel-less. Many of the projects don't use traditional gusset shaping; instead, a general increase of stitches (arch expansion) is worked near the heel shaping to provide the needed room for the arch.

THE WAY YOU WORK IT

Socks can be worked in several different directions. A sock knitter can begin at the cuff and work down to the heel, turn the corner (working the heel), and then work the foot and toe (called "cuff down," as in A Roll in the Hay, page 28). Alternately, in a process called "toe up," the knitter begins at the toe, works the foot, turns the corner, and then works up the leg and cuff, as in the Warm Up Socks, page 116. An explorative knitter might also work either from the cuff down or the toe up, skip the heel shaping, complete the sock, and then return to insert the skipped heel. This is a technique dubbed the "afterthought heel"; see Hot Waves (page 76) for an example of this method in action.

HUGGING THE CURVES

You'll get the most bang for your buck if you spend some time on heels and toes; these sock parts invite the most variety, creativity, and foot-hug-ability. The projects in this book demonstrate a number of different heel constructions, including standard (e.g. Puppy Love on page 93 and Rock-A-Bye on page 39), short row (e.g. Big Tease on page 90 and Cyber Flirt on page 165), and afterthought (e.g. Hot Waves on page 76 and Boyfriend Socks on page 48). A standard heel consists of a heel flap that lies down the back of the heel and a heel turn that wraps under the heel. A short row heel—which most resembles a commercial sock heel—consists of a series of progressively shorter short rows followed by an equivalent number of progressively longer short rows that form a cup for the heel (and may include a heel flap). Decidedly more impressive than its name, an afterthought heel is worked, in decreasing rounds, into an opening created when initially knitting the sock.

Toe constructions include standard (e.g., Make-Up Socks, page 67 and Snow Bunny, page 145), star (e.g., Spring Fling, page 138 and Quickie Socks, page 58), short row (e.g., Girl's Best Friend Thigh Highs, page 96 and Big Tease, page 90), and rectangle (e.g., Hot Waves, page 76). A standard toe is formed with paired decreases (cuff down) or increases (toe up) worked on either side of the toe. A star toe is formed with rounds of evenly spaced decreases. A short row toe is formed, like a short row heel, with a series of progressively shorter short rows followed by an equivalent number of progressively longer short rows. A rectangle toe is formed with a small rectangle of knitting, around which stitches are picked up and worked to begin the foot.

Does Size Matter?

It's an age-old question, and, when it comes to socks, the answer is yes and no. Knitted fabric stretches and is very forgiving. So, a sock of any size will fit a range of feet, within reason, of course. The most important dimensions of a sock are the leg length, foot length, foot circumference, and calf circumference (for taller socks). Your foot length is measured from the back of the heel to the tip of the longest toe. Foot circumference is measured around the widest part of the foot near the ball of the foot. The calf circumference is the distance around the widest part of the calf.

Most of the socks in this book are designed to fit women's feet, although some provide instructions for multiple sizes and others do not. In most designs, the leg length and foot length are easily altered by working fewer or more rounds. Work the leg until it measures the desired length. Work the foot until it measures 1½ to 2 inches (4 to 5 cm) less than desired foot length to allow for the toe (cuff down) or heel (toe up).

BIG SHOES? BIG FEET!

Nobody likes to be average, but it's nice to have some standard measurements to work with when you're making socks. Here's a handy chart (below) for average foot length and circumference measurements, along with standard shoe sizes.

SHOE SIZE (EURO)	FOOT LENGTH	FOOT CIRCUMFERENCE
Children's 4–6 (19–22)	4½–5½"/11.4–14cm	5½"/14cm
Children's 7–9 (23–25)	5½–6½"/14–16.5cm	6"/15.2cm
Children's 10–12 (27–30)	6½–7½"/16.5–19cm	6½"/16.5cm
Children's 13–3 (31–34)	7½–8½"/19–21.6cm	7¼"/18.4cm
Women's 3–5 (34–35)	8–9"/20.3–22.9cm	7½"/19cm
Women's 6–9 (37–40)	9–10"/22.9–25.4cm	8"/20.3cm
Women's 10–12 (41–44)	10–11"/25.4–27.9cm	8½"/21.6cm
Women's 13–14 (45–47)	11–12"/27.9–30.5cm	9¼"/23.5cm
Men's 4–7 (35–40)	9–10"/22.9–25.4cm	8"/20.3cm
Men's 8–10 (41–43)	10–11"/25.4–27.9cm	8½"/21.6cm
Men's 11–13 (44–47)	11–12"/27.9–30.5cm	8¾"/22.2cm
Men's 14–15 (11–49)	12–13"/30.5–33cm	9"/22.9cm

MAKING ADJUSTMENTS

Adjusting the foot or calf circumference of your knitted creation can be achieved in three ways. Thicker yarn or larger needles, thus a different gauge, will produce socks with a larger circumference, and thinner yarn or smaller needles will produce socks with a smaller circumference. Of course, you could also change both the yarn weight and the needle size. To check what circumference will be achieved by changing yarn thickness or needle size:

1 Knit a gauge swatch. Work in the round and use the appropriate pattern stitch. Measure the gauge swatch and determine the number of stitches per 4"/10cm.

2 Divide the number of stitches worked (at widest point of circumference) by the number of stitches of the gauge, and multiply the result by 4"/10cm. The result is the circumference if you work the socks with the different yarn or needles.

If changing the yarn or needle size is not an option (perhaps it would result in fabric that is too floppy or too stiff):

1 Measure the circumference of your foot (or calf).

2 Divide the circumference by 4"/10cm, and multiply the result by the stitch gauge (number of stitches per 4"/10cm). Round this number to the nearest stitch (or color) pattern multiple. This is the number of stitches that will need to be worked around the circumference of the foot to achieve the desired size. If the stitch pattern multiple is large, try inserting a small column of Stockinette stitch between repeats of the pattern.

Changing the number of stitches around the widest point of the foot or calf may also require adjusting the heel shaping and other parts of the sock. The number of heel stitches worked should be proportional to the number of stitches worked around the widest part of the foot. Use a proportion to determine a reasonable number of heel stitches to work. First, divide the new number of foot stitches by the old number of foot stitches. Multiply the result by the old number of heel stitches. Round this result for the new number of heel stitches needed.

Specific instructions for working the heel over the new number of stitches depend on the type of heel being worked.

Working a Standard Heel (cuff down)
Note: There are many variations on this technique.

Heel Flap: Work back and forth in rows over all stitches until flap is as long as desired.

Turn Heel:

Row 1: Work slightly more than one-half of the heel stitches (how many depends on the desired width for the back of the heel). Note the number of stitches left unworked, turn.

Row 2: Work across, leaving the same number of stitches unworked as were left in first row, turn.

Row 3: Work to one stitch before the gap formed by the turn of the previous row, decrease over the next stitch and the stitch following the gap, work one more stitch.

Repeat last row until all heel stitches have been worked.

Note: The last couple of repeats may not need to work an additional stitch following the decrease.

Working a Short Row Heel
Note: There are many variations on this technique.

Rows 1 and 2: Work to last heel st, wrap and turn.

Row 3: Work to 1 st before first wrapped st, wrap and turn.

Repeat last row until section of unwrapped stitches measures desired width for back of heel and there are an equal number of wrapped stitches on either side of the unwrapped stitches.

Next row: Work to first wrapped st, pick up the wrap and work it together with the st it wrapped.

Repeat last row until all wraps have been worked.

Sock Techniques

Whether you're a backseat-of-the-Mustang or an on-the-couch-in-front-of-the-television kind of knitter, you won't get very far in the sock world without the tools, tricks, and techniques of the trade.

USING YOUR TOOLS

No knitting kit would be complete without at least a few toys, and, thankfully, there's no shortage of sox paraphernalia out there. However, your most important tools are your needles. Socks are traditionally knit using four or five double-pointed needles. But don't feel bad if you want to explore a little: experimentation is good. Recent advances in materials have inspired new sock knitting techniques that use one or two circular needles.

knitting needle size chart

METRIC (mm)	US	UK/CANADIAN
2.0	0	14
2.25	1	13
2.75	2	12
3.0	-	11
3.25	3	10
3.5	4	-
3.75	5	9
4.0	6	8
4.5	7	7
5.0	8	6
5.5	9	5
6.0	10	4
6.5	10½	3
7.0	-	2
7.5	-	1
8.0	11	0
9.0	13	00
10.0	15	000
12.0	17	-
16.0	19	-
19.0	35	-
25.0	50	-

When you first join to knit in the round, lay your work on a flat surface so you can make sure you don't have a twist. If you have a twist, you'll have to start again. The first round is the trickiest, but it gets easier after that.

DPNs, Baby!

Double-pointed needles are the physical embodiment of sock efficiency, although all those pointy ends can feel a little sadistic at times. Cast on to one needle, distribute the stitches over three or four needles, and arrange the needles in a ring. With an additional needle—the working needle—work the stitches from the first needle. The newly empty needle then becomes the working needle. Use the working needle to work the stitches from the next needle, and so on, until all stitches on all needles have been worked, and a round has been completed.

Here's how: One or two needles hold the front of the leg (or instep) stitches, and two needles hold the back of the leg (or sole or heel) stitches. The first needle to be worked is needle #1, and the remaining needles are numbered, in increasing order, clockwise. Each round of knitting instructions specifies how all the stitches on all the needles are to be worked (e.g. Round 2: Knit.) or how the stitches on each of the three or four needles are to be worked (e.g. Round 2: Needle #1: K to last 3 sts, ssk, k1; Needle #2: K1, k2tog, k to last 3 sts, ssk, k1; Needle #3: K1, k2tog, k to end).

Soxpert Secret #17:

"Ladders" are a vertical series of holes that result because the gap between the double-pointed needles places tension on the stitches on each side of the gap, thus loosening them. To avoid holes and ladders, take care to pull tightly when working the last stitch on one needle and the first stitch on the next needle. Also, using five double-pointed needles, rather than four, spreads the stitch tension more evenly between needles, helping reduce the formation of holes between needles.

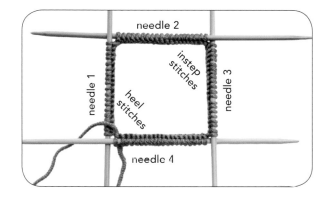

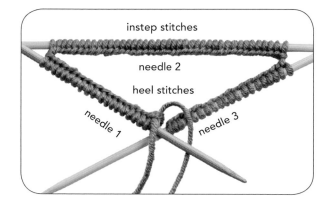

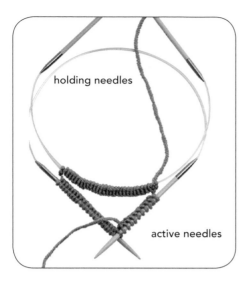

holding needles

active needles

Two Circulars: Twice the Fun!

In the mood for something a little less conventional? Try working with two 24"/61cm circular needles. Cast on to one needle, and then slide one-half of the stitches onto the other needle. Hold the stitches (the set of stitches with the working yarn attached) on the cable of one needle—the holding needle—and allow the tips to dangle behind the work. Work the stitches on the other needle, called the active needle. When all the stitches on the active needle have been worked, slide them to the cable and allow the tips to dangle. Rotate the work clockwise, bringing the other needle to the front. Slide the held stitches to the tip of the needle, and work these stitches to complete a round.

Soxpert Secret #48:

Use needles of different lengths or colors to make them easy to distinguish. Take care to always work with opposite ends of the same needle (the needle on which the stitches lie).

Here's how: One needle holds the front of the leg (or instep) stitches, and the other holds the back of the leg (or sole or heel) stitches. The needles may be numbered, needle #1 and needle #2 (or needles A and B). Each round of knitting instructions specifies how all the stitches on all the needles are to be worked (e.g. Round 2: Knit) or how stitches on each of the two needles are to be worked (e.g. Round 2: Needle #1: Work in instep pattern across; Needle #2: Knit).

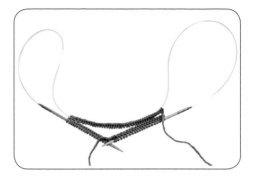

Rules for the Solo Circular

Are you a quick-and-dirty kind of knitter? Using a single long circular needle, the magic loop method might be for you. Cast on to the needle. Gently pull the cable out from the midpoint of the stitches, forming a large loop and leaving one-half of the stitches lying on each end of the cable. Leave one set of stitches (the set of stitches with the working yarn attached) on the cable, and slide the other set of stitches onto the tip. Draw out enough of the cable to work comfortably (forming another loop), and work the set of stitches from the tip. Slide the recently worked stitches to the cable, rotate the work (bringing the unworked stitches to the front), and slide the unworked stitches onto the tip. Draw out enough of the cable to work comfortably, and work this set of stitches to complete a round.

Soxpert Secret #73:

Flexibility is important! Be sure to use a circular needle with a very long—between 32"/81.5cm and 40"/101.5cm—and flexible cable.

Here's how: One set of stitches is the front of the leg (or instep) stitches, and the other set is the back of the leg (or sole or heel stitches). Since there is only one needle, it is not numbered. Each round of knitting instructions specifies how all the stitches are to be worked (e.g. Round 2: Knit) or how each set of stitches are to be worked (e.g. Round 2: Work in instep pattern across instep sts, slide stitches, knit across heel sts) and may indicate when the sets of stitches need to be redistributed between the cable and the tip.

Mixing Things Up

A little variety can help spice up your sox life. Sometimes it's best to use a combination of needle techniques—as in Blue Crush (page 122) and Golden Dahlia (page 156)—to get the best of both worlds. In either case, the project instructions specify whether double-pointed needles, two circular needles, or a single circular needle are needed. However, any of the projects can be worked using any of the needle techniques, so you can always work with what you've got.

Double-pointed needle instructions worked on one or two circular needles: Work the instructions for the heel over the stitches on one of the two circular needles or one set of stitches on the single circular needle. Work the instructions for the instep stitches over the stitches on the second of the two circular needles or the other set of stitches on the single circular needle.

Soxpert Secret #14:

To stay oriented, place markers to indicate the beginning of the set of stitches associated with each double-pointed needle.

Circular needle instructions worked on double-pointed needles: Work the instructions for one of the two circular needles, or one set of stitches on the single circular needle, on stitches distributed evenly over two double-pointed needles. Work the instructions for the second of the two circular needles, or the other set of stitches on the single circular needle, on stitches distributed evenly over two more double-pointed needles.

Two circular needle instructions worked on one circular needle: Work one set of stitches on the single circular needle in the same manner as stitches on one of the two circular needles. Work the other set of stitches on the single circular needle in the same manner as stitches on the second of the two circular needles.

One circular needle instructions worked on two circular needles: Work the stitches on one circular needle in the same manner as one set of stitches on the single circular needle. Work the stitches on the second circular needle in the same manner as the other set of stitches on the single circular needle.

SOCKTALK

“ I talk about sock knitting to anyone and everyone…regardless of their interest or lack thereof. I can probably guess the yarn brand, color name, and pattern in a finished pair of socks before I read the details. And I have more sock yarn in my stash than all other yarns combined…and then some. ”

STAR ATHENA on . . . sock obsession

If there's a sensual part of a sock, and we're pretty sure there is, it's got to be the yarn. Socks have been made from almost every imaginable fiber—from flax to cotton, alpaca to silk, and acrylic to latex—in various degrees of tactile appeal. But, of course, it's not all about pleasing the fingers. Sock yarns are selected for durability, warmth, absorbency, elasticity, and beauty. Wool is one of the warmest fibers, while acrylic is one of the most durable. Cotton is highly absorbent, alpaca is seriously soft, and silk reflects color beautifully. And the choices continue; modern sock yarn blends combine the best qualities of several fibers to achieve every desirable characteristic. For an extra foot-hugging fit, a thin strand of elastic can be worked along with a strand of yarn to provide additional stretch and strength to the cuffs, heel, or toes of socks.

The weight (or thickness) of yarn has a profound effect on the process and result of knitted socks. The standard yarn weight system groups yarns into seven weight categories: 0-lace, 1-superfine, 2-fine, 3-light, 4-medium, 5-bulky, and 6-super bulky. The majority of socks are knit with yarn weights ranging from 0 to 4.

0-lace weight (10 count thread): Not afraid of commitment? Built for comfort—not for speed—this weight requires the use of very thin needles and a large number of stitches; you're going to have to take your sweet time. This yarn yields lightweight socks with that "barely there" feel.

1-superfine (fingering or sock weight): Tried and true. As the name "sock weight" suggests, this weight is frequently used for knitting socks. It produces a light yet sturdy fabric for a product that's, dare we say, "dependable."

2-fine (sport or baby): Wishing for socks with a little athletic prowess? Sport weight yarn allows for a little more speed and strength, allowing you to really go the distance. This slightly thicker yarn works up quickly on larger needles with a smaller number of stitches and yields a sock with a bit more "oomph."

3-light (double knit or light worsted): Want to have your cake and eat it too? Light worsted weight yarn can provide the speed and strength of sport weight yarn, but the result is a sleeker sock. Think velour track suit: sporty, yes, but who runs in velour?

4-medium (worsted): Looking for a quickie? This weight works up very quickly with large needles and few stitches. Socks made with worsted weight yarn are perfect for cushion and warmth, and you don't have to feel guilty the next morning.

YARN STANDARDS CHART

YARN WEIGHT SYMBOL & CATEGORY NAMES	(0) lace	(1) super fine	(2) fine	(3) light	(4) medium	(5) bulky	(6) super bulky
TYPE OF YARNS IN CATEGORY	Fingering 10-count crochet thread	Sock, Fingering, Baby	Sport, Baby	DK, Light Worsted	Worsted, Afghan, Aran	Chunky, Craft, Rug	Bulky, Roving

Source: Craft Yarn Council of America's www.YarnStandards.com

CASTING ON/GETTING IT ON

So, you're primed, ready, and in the mood for a little sock making. Time to get started, but don't rush things with a kinky cast on. Many of these projects will work using any basic cast-on technique, including long tail, knit-on, cable, and backwards loop/e-wrap. If a particular cast-on technique is not specified in the project instructions, use the technique that you like.

Provisional Cast-On Techniques

A provisional cast on allows a knitter to easily work into the stitches along the opposite side of the cast-on edge. This technique is useful when working a fold-over cuff (as in Lotus, page 124) or working a toe-up sock like Big Tease (page 90). There are a number of other provisional cast-on techniques, any of which may be used in projects that do not specify a particular provisional cast on. Here are two specific provisional cast-on methods that you might not have worked with before.

Waste Yarn Provisional Cast On

Use a length of waste yarn to work the first round. Work the next round with the project yarn. When the stitches along the opposite side of the cast-on edge are needed, carefully remove the waste yarn exposing the stitches, and slip the exposed stitches onto needles.

You can also use the waste yarn technique to easily work into a section of stitches in the middle of a piece, for example, when you're working an afterthought heel. Work the waste yarn in the desired location, then resume work with the project yarn, first working across the stitches of the waste yarn. When the stitches around the waste yarn are needed, carefully remove the waste yarn to expose the stitches, and slip the exposed stitches onto needles.

Chained Cast On

Use a crochet hook and waste yarn to make a length of chains. Make two more chains that the number of stitches to be cast on. Beginning in the second chain, pick up one stitch in each chain until the desired number of stitches has been placed on needles. As with the waste yarn cast on, when the stitches along the opposite side of the cast-on edge are needed, carefully remove the waste yarn chain, expose the stitches, and slip the exposed stitches onto needles.

turkish cast on

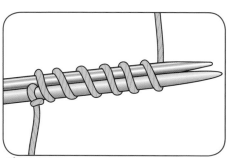

step one

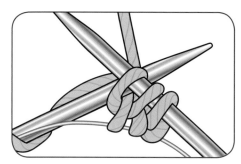

step two

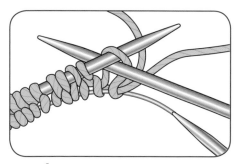

step three

Toe-Up Cast-On Techniques

Some knitters like the slow buildup of working from the toe up the leg. There are specific cast-on techniques particularly suited for the toe-up method. All of the following cast-on techniques can be worked with circular or double-pointed needles.

Turkish Cast On

Hold two needles in your left hand, one on top of the other. Make a slip knot with the working yarn and place it on the lower needle. Wrap the working yarn back underneath the needles, up and over the top of the needles, and back down to the bottom (this is your first stitch). Continue wrapping yarn around your set of needles until the correct number of stitches are placed; each needle holds one half of the total number of stitches (step 1). Pull the lower needle through the stitches so they are sitting on the end of the needle (or on the cable of 1 or 2 circulars). Knit the stitches of the upper needle as written in the pattern (step 2). Flip work so that the lower and upper needles are switched. Pull the lower needle through the stitches so they are sitting on the end of the needle (or on the cable of 1 or 2 circulars). Pull the upper needle through the stitches so the stitches are ready to be knit (step 3). Remove the slip knot, and knit the stitches of the upper needle as written in the pattern.

Figure-8 Cast On

Hold two needles in your left hand, one on top of the other. Hold the yarn against the lower needle, and bring the yarn between the two needles, from front to back. Wrap the yarn up and over the upper needle and back between the two needles, from front to back. Bring the yarn under and over the lower needle, from back to front, and bring the yarn between the two needles. Repeat this process until you have cast on the number of stitches desired; each needle holds one-half of the total number of stitches. The process should end with the yarn between the two needles and the lower needle being the last needle wrapped (steps 1 and 2). Work the first round of stitches beginning with stitches on the upper needle (step 3). Flip the work when you reach the end of one needle, then work the stitches on the next needle. The stitches on the lower needle will be twisted, so work these stitches through the back loop on the first round.

Note: You may wish to tighten the stitches on the lower needle before working round 1 on these stitches. Tighten them, one by one, as you would your shoelaces.

figure-8 cast on

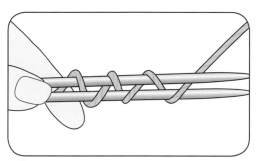

step one

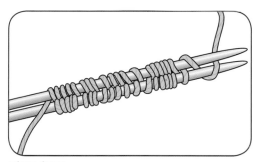

step two

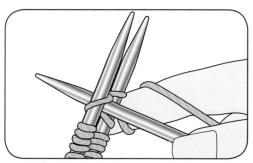

step three

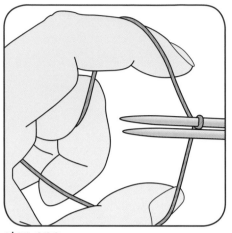

step one

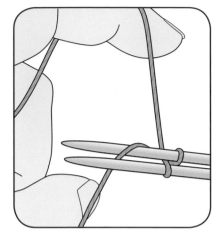

step two

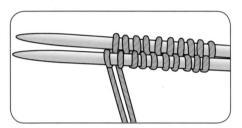

step three

Magic Cast On

Leaving a long tail (long enough to cast on one-half of the stitches), place a slip knot on one needle. Hold two needles in your right hand, one on top of the other, with the slip knot on the upper needle (the slip knot is the first stitch cast on the upper needle). Hold the tail and working yarn in your left hand. Hold the tail above the needles (upper strand) and the working yarn below the needles (lower strand) (step 1). Wrap the tail of the yarn under the lower needle, from back to front, then in front of the needle and back between the two needles (one stitch cast onto lower needle). Wrap the working yarn over the upper needle, from back to front, then in front of the needle and back between the two needles (one more stitch cast onto the upper needle) (step 2). Continue alternating wrap-

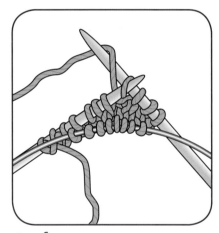

step four

ping the lower needle with the tail (upper strand), and wrapping the upper needle with the working yarn (lower strand), until desired number of stitches have been cast on (step 3). To begin first round, drop tail and turn needles so that lower needle is now on top (needle #1). Ensure that the tail is between needle #1 and the working yarn. Work the first round of stitches beginning with stitches on needle #1 (step 4). The stitches on needle #2 will be twisted, so work these stitches through the back loop on the first round.

Risky Knits?

Exactly how adventurous are you, in knitting terms that is? Take this quick quiz and total your points to see if you're a timid knitter or a twisted temptress.

How many different "special someones" have you knit projects for in the past year? (Count one point for each recipient.)

What type of yarn do you use most often to make socks for yourself?
Cotton (Ol' reliable.) (1 point)
Chenille (Looks good and feels good.) (2 points)
Cashmere (Oooh-la-la, and then some.) (3 points)

How many articles of knitted lingerie have you clocked in your knitting career? (Count one point for each article.)

What's your favorite yarn weight for making socks?
Dk—Socks in a hurry! (3 points)
Fingering weight—Tried and true. (1 point)
Extra fine—Slow and steady…and a little bit fancy. (2 points)

Tame-o, Lame-o—1 to 3 points
Hate to break it to you, but, on a scale of one to risky knitter, you score a cold fish. You tend toward the mild side of life and knitting…those fingerless gloves just seem a little too bohemian for your tastes.

Medium Spice—4-7 points
If you were a knitting salsa, you'd be medium. A tad adventurous but just shy of hot, you're a middle-of-the-road kind of knitter. You don't do cutesy, but, let's face it, knitted bikinis make you cringe.

Sock Explorer Extraordinaire—8+ points
Whoa, baby! You're ready for adventure—knitting bag in tow, of course—leaving no knitting taboo unexplored. Cabled handcuffs? Bring it on.

THE GRAND FINALE: BINDING OFF

Make sure your socks end happily with the appropriate bind-off technique. When working cuff-down socks, use a sewn bind off such as Kitchener Stitch or a stretchy sewn bind off. A 3-needle bind off, worked from the wrong side of the sock as in Puppy Love (page 93), is another toe-finishing option. When working toe-up socks, any common bind off worked loosely (consider using a larger needle) and in pattern will usually suffice.

Stretchy Sewn Bind Off

Cut your yarn, leaving a tail that is four times longer than your bind-off edge. Thread the tail onto a yarn needle and hold the work with right side facing you. The yarn should come from the left. Work as follows: *keeping the working yarn above, insert the needle through the first two stitches on the knitting needle as if to purl, then sew through the first stitch on the knitting needle as if to knit. Drop the first stitch off the knitting needle; repeat from * until all stitches are bound off.

sewn bind off

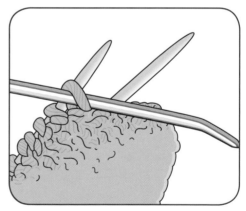

step one   step two

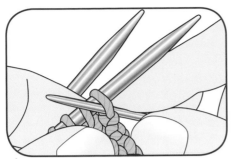

step one

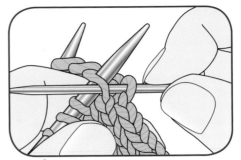

step four

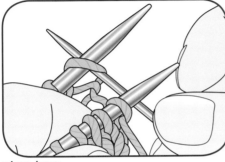

step two

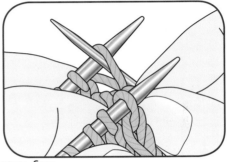

step five

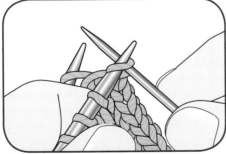

step three

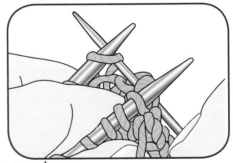

step six

Kitchener Stitch Bind Off

Thread the long tail onto a tapestry needle. With the wrong sides together, hold both knitting needles together and even, insert the tapestry needle into the first stitch on front needle as if to purl, and draw yarn through. Leave st on needle. Hold the yarn in the back, insert the tapestry needle as if to knit into the first stitch on the back needle, and draw the yarn through. Leave the stitch on needle. Hold the yarn in front, insert the tapestry needle as if to knit through the first stitch on the front needle, and draw the yarn through. Slip the stitch off the needle. Insert the tapestry needle through the next stitch on the front needle as if to purl, and draw the yarn through. Leave the stitch on the needle. Insert the tapestry needle as if to purl through the first stitch on the back needle, and draw the yarn through. Slip the stitch off the needle. Insert the tapestry needle through the next stitch on the back needle as if to knit, and draw the yarn through. Leave the stitch on the needle. Repeat the last two steps until all but one stitch has been eliminated. Draw the yarn through this stitch to secure.

Cables

C2B: Cable 2 back – Slip 1 stitch onto cable needle and hold in back, k1, k1 from cable needle.

C2F: Cable 2 front – Slip 1 stitch onto cable needle and hold in front, k1, k1 from cable needle.

RT: Right Twist – Skip the first stitch, knit into 2nd stitch, then knit skipped stitch. Slip both stitches from needle together OR k2tog leaving stitches on left needle, then k first stitch again. Slip both stitches off needle.

C2Bp: Cable 2 back purl – Slip 1 stitch onto cable needle and hold in back, k1, p1 from cable needle.

C2Fp: Cable 2 front purl – Slip 1 stitch onto cable needle and hold in front, p1, k1 from cable needle.

C3B: Cable 3 back – Slip 2 stitches onto cable needle and hold in back, k1, k2 from cable needle.

C3F: Cable 3 front – Slip 1 stitch onto cable needle and hold in front, k2, k1 from cable needle.

C3Bp: Cable 3 back purl – Slip 1 stitch onto cable needle and hold in back, k2, p1 from cable needle.

C3Fp: Cable 3 front purl – Slip 2 stitches onto cable needle and hold in front, p1, k2 from cable needle.

C4B: Cable 4 back – Slip 2 stitches onto cable needle and hold in back, k2, k2 from cable needle.

C4F: Cable 4 front – Slip 2 stitches onto cable needle and hold in front, k2, k2 from cable needle.

C5Fp: Cable 5 front purl – Slip 3 stitches onto cable needle and hold in front, k2, (p1, k2) from cable needle.

dec: decreas(e)(ing)(s)

k: knit

k2tog: Knit 2 stitches together.

k3tog: Knit 3 stitches together.

kfb: Knit in front and back of stitch (increase).

inc: increas(e)(ing)(s)

m1: make 1

On RS (m1k): make 1 knit: Insert right needle from back to front under the strand between two stitches, lift this loop onto left needle and knit into the back of the loop.

On WS (m1p): make 1 purl: Insert right needle from back to front under the strand between two stitches, lift this loop onto left needle and purl into the front of the loop.

p: purl

pfb: Purl in front and back of stitch (increase).

p2tog: Purl 2 stitches together.

sl: slip

skp: Slip 1 stitch, knit, pass slipped stitch over.

sk2p: Slip1 stitch, k2tog, pass slipped stitch over.

S2kp2: Slip 2 stitches as if to knit 2 stitches together, knit 1, pass both slipped stitches over (2 stitches decreased).

ssk: slip, slip, knit – Slip 1 stitch as if to knit, slip next stitch as if to knit. Insert left needle through the front loops of the two slipped stitches and knit them together.

ssp: slip, slip, purl – Slip 1 stitch as if to purl, slip next stitch as if to knit, slip both stitches back to left-hand needle and p2tog through back loop.

sssk: slip, slip, slip, knit 3 slipped stitches together.

st(s): stitch(es)

St st: Stockinette stitch

tbl: through back loop

w&t: wrap and turn

(RS) Move the yarn to the front of the work (between the needles), slip the next stitch, move the yarn to the back of the work (between the needles), slip the stitch back onto the left needle, turn.

(WS) Move the yarn to the back of the work, slip the next stitch, move the yarn to the front of the work, slip the stitch back onto the left needle, turn.

wyib: with yarn in back

wyif: with yarn in front

Keeping It Clean

If you want your socks to last a long time, you'll have to put in a little extra work. Many yarn labels provide washing instructions, so save the label or note the fiber content and the recommended cleaning and drying instructions. With sock cleaning, a gentle hand is best; never use harsh chemicals, extreme temperatures, or methods other than those suggested on the yarn label. Prior to washing, remove any non-washable trims and make any needed repairs, as cleaning can enlarge a hole and unravel loose hems.

Soxpert Secret #4

Rather than laying your socks flat to dry, place them over appropriate-sized sock blockers to make sure they retain their size and shape. Sock blockers are available for purchase or you can make your own using carefully bent wire coat hangers, plastic canvas, or other materials.

and now, slip into something comfortable,

and enjoy yourself...

A Roll in the Hay

So named for their attractive wheat sheaves stitch pattern, these socks are a joyful combination of soft, supple texture and come-hither hues.

by GINA HOUSE

SKILL LEVEL
Intermediate

FINISHED MEASUREMENTS
Foot circumference 8½"/21.5cm

Leg length 8"/20.5cm

Foot length 7½ (9½)"/19 (24)cm

MATERIALS AND TOOLS
Approx total: 400yd/360m of (1) fingering weight yarn, superwash wool/bamboo/nylon blend, in gold

Knitting needles: 2.75mm (size 2 U.S.) set of 5 double-pointed needles, *or size to obtain gauge*

Stitch markers (optional)

Stitch holder (optional)

Cable needle

Yarn needle

GAUGE
30 sts and 40 rows = 4"/10cm in Stockinette Stitch (knit every round)

Always take time to check your gauge.

CUFF
Cast on 68 sts onto one needle. Distribute the stitches evenly over four needles (17 sts per needle). Place a stitch marker for beginning of round. Taking care not to twist stitches, join to work in the round.

Work in K2, p2 Rib pattern for 2"/5cm.

LEG
Round 1 (set–up round): K2tog, p2tog, k2tog, (p2, k2) 3 times, p2, m1, p1, m1, p2tog, p1, (k2, p2) 3 times, kfb, k1, (p2, k2) 3 times, p2, m1, p1, m1, p2tog, p1, (k2, p2) 3 times—68 sts.

Round 2: *(K1, p1, k1); work row 2 of Modified Wheat Sheaves pattern; repeat from * around.

Rounds 3–40: *(K1, p1, k1); work next row of Modified Wheat Sheaves pattern; repeat from * around—64 sts.

Round 41 (transition round): P2, k1, p2, (k2, p2) 3 times, (m1, k1, m1), (p2, k2) 2 times, p2, (k2tog) twice, (p2, k1, p2), (k2, p2) 3 times, m1; continue with a different needle as follows: k1, m1, (p2, k2) twice, p2, (k2tog) twice, keep working with same needle and continue in pattern over next 19 stitches from the first needle.

You should now have 33 sts on last needle used (for instep) and 31 sts (total) on other needles (for heel).

HEEL FLAP
Work back and forth over 31 heel sts only. If desired, place instep stitches on a stitch holder or waste yarn.

Row 1 (RS): Sl 1, k2tog, *(sl 1, k1); repeat from * across—30 sts.

Row 2 (WS): Sl 1, purl across.

Row 3: *Sl 1, k1; repeat from * across.

Row 4: Sl 1, purl across.

Repeat last two rows 13 more times or until heel flap measures approx 2"/5cm.

modified wheat sheaves pattern (multiples of 15 sts + 14)

Row 1: (P2, k2) 3 times, p2, m1, p1, m1, p2, (k2, p2) 3 times.

Row 2: (P2, k2) 3 times, p2, k1, p1, k1, p2, (k2, p2) 3 times.

Row 3: (P2, k2) 3 times, p2, m1, p1, k1, p1, m1, p2, (k2, p2) 3 times.

Row 4: (P2, k2) 3 times, p2, (k1, p1) twice, k1, p2, (k2, p2) 3 times.

Row 5: (P2, k2) 3 times, p2, m1, (p1, k1) twice, p1, m1, p2, (k2, p2) 3 times.

Row 6: (P2, k2) 3 times, p2, (k1, p1) 3 times, k1, p2, (k2, p2) 3 times.

Row 7: (P2, k2) 3 times, p2, m1, (p1, k1) 3 times, p1, m1, p2, (k2, p2) 3 times.

Row 8: (P2, k2) 3 times, p2, (k1, p1) 4 times, k1, p2, (k2, p2) 3 times.

Row 9: (P2, k2) 3 times, p2, m1, (p1, k1) 4 times, p1, m1, p2, (k2, p2) 3 times.

Row 10: P1, pfb, sl 10 sts as if to purl wyif, pass first slipped st over the other 9 slipped sts, p2, (k1, p1) 5 times, k1; end 2nd repeat with p2 instead of k1.

Row 11: (P2, k2) 3 times, p2, ssk, (p1, k1) 3 times, p1, k2tog, p2, (k2, p2) 3 times.

Row 12: (P2, k2) 3 times, p2, (k1, p1) 4 times, k1, p2, (k2, p2) 3 times.

Row 13: (P2, k2) 3 times, p2, ssk, (p1, k1) 2 times, p1, k2tog, p2, (k2, p2) 3 times.

Row 14: (P2, k2) 3 times, p2, (k1, p1) 3 times, k1, p2, (k2, p2) 3 times.

Row 15: (P2, k2) 3 times, p2, ssk, p1, k1, p1, k2tog, p2, (k2, p2) 3 times.

Row 16: (P2, k2) 3 times, p2, (k1, p1) 2 times, k1, p2, (k2, p2) 3 times.

Row 17: (P2, k2) 3 times, p2, ssk, p1, k2tog, p2, (k2, p2) 3 times.

Row 18: (P2, k2) 3 times, p2, k1, p1, k1, p2, (k2, p2) 3 times.

Row 19: (P2, k2) 3 times, p2, sk2p, p2, (k2, p2) 3 times.

Row 20: (P2, k2) 3 times, p2, k1, p2, (k2, p2) 3 times.

Repeat rows 1–20 for Modified Wheat Sheaves pattern.

Turn Heel

Continue to work back and forth on heel stitches only.

Row 1 (RS): Sl 1, k16, ssk, k1, turn.

Row 2 (WS): Sl 1, p5, p2tog, p1, turn.

Row 3: Sl 1, k6, ssk, k1, turn.

Row 4: Sl 1, p7, p2tog, p1, turn.

Continue working in this manner working one additional stitch before the decrease on each row, until 18 stitches remain, ending with a WS row.

Pick-up round: With RS of heel facing and spare needle, sl 1, k8 heel sts; with another needle k9 remaining heel sts, pick up and k15 sts along side of heel flap, pick up and k1 st in the corner (needle #1); work row 2 of Modified Wheat Sheaves pattern across instep stitches (needles #2 and #3); with another needle, pick up and k1 st in the corner, pick up and k15 sts along the opposite side of heel flap, k sts from spare needle (needle #4)—83 sts (25 sts each on needles #1 and #4, and 33 sts over needles #2 and #3).

Shape Gusset

Round 1:

Needle #1: Knit to last 3 sts, k2tog, k1—24 sts;

Needles #2 and #3: Continue in established Modified Wheat Sheaves pattern—33 sts;

Needle #4: K1, ssk, knit to end—24 sts.

Round 2:

Needle #1: Knit;

Needles #2 and #3: Continue in established Modified Wheat Sheaves pattern;

Needle #4: Knit.

Repeat last 2 rounds until 65 stitches remain (33 instep stitches, and 32 heel stitches).

Repeat round 2 only, beginning with row 1 of Modified Wheat Sheaves pattern, until rows 1–20 of Modified Wheat Sheaves pattern have been worked once (twice) more. End ready to work stitches from needle #1.

Shape Toe
Round 1:

Needle #1: Knit to last 3 sts, k2tog, k1—15 sts;

Needles #2 and #3: K1, ssk, k12, k2tog, k12, k2tog, k1—30 sts;

Needle #4: K1, ssk, knit to end—15 sts (60 sts total).

Round 2: Knit.

Round 3:

Needle #1: Knit to last 3 sts, k2tog, k1—14 sts;

Needles #2 and #3: K1, ssk, knit to last 3 sts, k2tog, k1—28 sts;

Needle #4: K1, ssk, knit to end—14 sts.

Repeat last two rounds until 20 total stitches remain (5 sts each on needles #1 and #4, 10 sts over needles #2 and #3. End with round 2.

Finish Toe
Knit stitches of needle #1 onto needle #4, and slip stitches from needle #2 onto needle #3 (two sets of 10 stitches each on two needles). Cut yarn, leaving a 20"/51cm tail. Use Kitchener Stitch to sew the two sets of 10 stitches together.

FINISHING
Weave in ends.

This project was knit with:

Sereknity SockOptions' Shimmer Sock, 1 fingering weight, 60% superwash merino, 30% bamboo, 10% nylon, 3.75oz/106g = approx 400yd/360m per skein 1 skein, pharaohs gold colorway

49% of sock knitters wear socks to bed.

modified wheat sheaves pattern

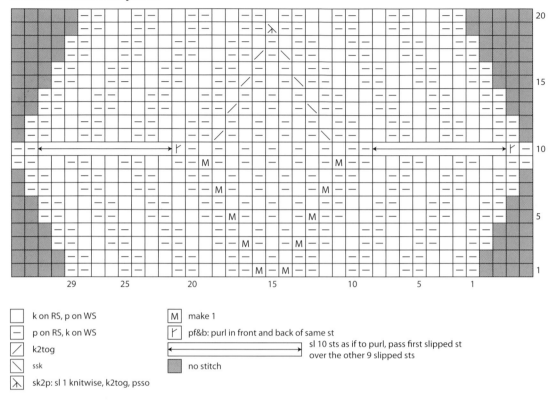

	k on RS, p on WS		M	make 1
	p on RS, k on WS		⌐	pf&b: purl in front and back of same st
/	k2tog			sl 10 sts as if to purl, pass first slipped st over the other 9 slipped sts
\	ssk			
人	sk2p: sl 1 knitwise, k2tog, psso			no stitch

SKILL LEVEL
Intermediate

FINISHED MEASUREMENTS
Foot circumference 8½"/22cm

Leg length 8½"/22cm

Foot length 10"/25cm

MATERIALS AND TOOLS
Approx total: 490yd/448m of **(1)** fingering weight yarn, wool/nylon

Color A: 315yd/288m of **(1)** fingering weight yarn, wool/nylon, in multi-blue

Color B: 175yd/160m of **(1)** fingering weight yarn, wool/nylon, in spring green

Knitting needles: 3.25mm (size 3 U.S.) set of 4 double-pointed needles, *or size to obtain gauge*

Stitch holder

Stitch marker

Yarn needle

GAUGE
30 sts and 36 rows = 4"/10cm in Stockinette Stitch (knit every round)

Always take time to check your gauge.

Two to Tango

A little tropical salsa anyone? These lively fish-themed socks—complete with a wave-inspired design—will make you feel light on your feet. Aye carumba!

by LINDSAY OBERMEYER

CUFF

With A, cast on 66 sts. Distribute the stitches evenly over three needles (22 sts per needle). Place a stitch marker for beginning of round. Taking care not to twist stitches, join to work in the round.

Rounds 1 and 3: Knit.

Rounds 2 and 4: Purl.

Round 5: Knit.

Round 6: *K2tog, k2, kfb in next 2 sts, k3, ssk; repeat from * to end.

Rounds 7–12: Repeat rounds 5 and 6 three times.

Rounds 13–24: Repeat rounds 1–12.

Rounds 25–29: Repeat rounds 1–5.

Round 30: K31, ssk, k31, ssk—64 sts.

Rounds 31 and 32: Knit.

Work all rounds of Fish Chart 4 times.

HEEL FLAP

Set-up: K16, turn; p32, turn.

Heel is worked back and forth on the first 32 sts only. Place remaining sts on a st holder (for instep).

Row 1 (RS): With B, *sl 1 wyib as if to purl, k1; repeat from * across.

Row 2 (WS): With B, *p1, sl 1 wyif as if to purl; repeat from * across.

Row 3: With A, *k1, sl 1 wyib as if to purl; repeat from * across.

Row 4: With A, *sl 1 wyif as if to purl, p1; repeat from * across.

Repeat last 4 rows 7 more times (for a total of 32 rows). Cut B leaving a long tail to weave in later, continue with A.

Turn Heel

Row 1 (RS): K18, ssk, k1, turn.

Row 2: Sl 1 as if to purl, p5, p2tog, p1, turn.

Row 3: Sl 1 as if to purl, knit to 1 st before gap, ssk (1 st from each side of gap), k1, turn.

Row 4: Sl 1 as if to purl, purl to 1 st before gap, p2tog (1 st from each side of gap), p1, turn.

Repeat last 2 rows until all heel stitches have been worked, ending with a WS row—18 sts.

Note: On the last 2 rows, there will be no extra stitch to work after the decrease.

GUSSET

Redistribute stitches as follows: With RS of heel facing, with needle #1 knit across all heel sts, pick up and knit tbl (twisting the stitches) 16 sts along side of heel flap; with needle #2 k32 instep sts from stitch holder; with needle #3 pick up and knit tbl 16 sts along side of heel flap, then k9 sts from needle #1—82 sts (25 sts on needle #1, 32 sts on needle #2, and 25 sts on needle #3).

Note: The round now begins at the center back of heel.

Round 1:

Needle #1: Knit to last 3 sts, k2tog, k1—24 sts.

Needle #2: Knit—32 sts.

Needle #3: K1, ssk, knit to end—24 sts.

Round 2: Knit all sts on all needles.

Round 3: Repeat round 1–78 sts.

Repeat last 2 rounds 7 more times—64 sts (16 sts each on needles #1 and #3, 32 sts on needle #2).

FOOT

Round 1: With A, knit.

Round 2: With A, *p1, k3; repeat from * around.

Round 3: With B, k1, sl 3 wyib, *k3, sl 3 wyib; repeat from * around.

Round 4: With B, p1, k1, *sl 1 wyib, k5; repeat from * to last 2 sts, sl 1 wyib, p1.

Round 5: With B, knit.

Round 6: With B, p4, *k3, p3; repeat from * around.

Round 7: With A, k4, *sl 3 wyib, k3; repeat from * around.

Round 8: With A, p1, k4, *sl 1 wyib, k5; repeat from * to last 5 sts, sl 1 wyib, k4.

Repeat last 8 rounds 6 more times (you will see seven "stripes" of B).

Shape Toe

Round 1: *With A k1, with B k1; repeat from * around.

Round 2:

Needle #1: Knit to last 3 sts, k2tog, k1—15 sts.

Needle #2: K1, ssk, knit to last 3 sts, k2tog, k1—30 sts.

Needle #3: K1, ssk, knit to end—15 sts.

Round 3: Knit, keeping in established stripe pattern.

Repeat last 2 rounds until 32 sts (8 sts each on needles #1 and #3, 16 sts on needle #2).

Repeat round 2 only until 8 sts remain (2 sts each on needles #1 and #3, 4 sts on needle #2).

Finish Toe

Knit stitches from needle #1 onto needle #3 (4 sts each on two needles).

Cut yarn, leaving an 18"/46cm tail of yarn on far right of needle and a shorter tail of other color to weave in later. Use Kitchener Stitch to sew the two sets of stitches together.

FINISHING

Weave in ends.

This project was knit with:

Lorna's Laces' Shepherd Sock Yarn, fingering weight, 80% superwash wool, 20% nylon, 2oz/57g = approx 215yd/197m per hank
(A) 2 hanks, #407 devon
(B) 1 hank, #47 carol green

off the charts

fish chart

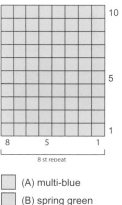

8 st repeat

☐ (A) multi-blue
☐ (B) spring green

35

Going out or staying in, you're bound to hit it out of the park with these bold baseball-inspired socks. And after one spin on the dance floor in these babies, you may never knit socks with toes and heels again.

by CATHY CARRON

Takeout for Two

LEG #1
Beginning at the foot, with D, cast on 40 (48) sts. Distribute the sts evenly over four double-pointed needles (10 (12) sts per needle). Taking care not to twist stitches, join to work in the round.

Work in K2, p2 Rib pattern until piece measures 3½ (5)"/9 (13)cm from beginning.

Make Heel Opening
Next round: Bind off 22 (26) sts, continue in K2, p2 Rib around.

Next round: Cast on 22 (26) sts, continue in K2, p2 Rib around.

Work in K2, p2 Rib for 12 (16) more rounds.

SKILL LEVEL
Easy

FINISHED MEASUREMENTS
Foot circumference 8 (9½)"/20.5 (24)cm

Calf circumference 12 (14½)"/30.5 (37)cm

Leg length 23 (25½)"/58 (65)cm

Foot length (toeless) 3½ (5)"/9 (12.5)cm

MATERIALS AND TOOLS
Approx total: 675 (770)yd/608 (693)m of **2** sport weight yarn, alpaca

Color A: 200 (220)yd/180 (198)m of **2** sport weight yarn, alpaca, in dark gray

Color B: 200 (220)yd/180 (198)m of **2** sport weight yarn, alpaca, in medium gray

Color C: 200 (220)yd/180 (198)m of **2** sport weight yarn, alpaca, in light gray

Color D: 75 (110)yd/68 (99)m of **2** sport weight yarn, alpaca, in red

Knitting needles: 3.5mm (size 4 U.S.) set of 5 double-pointed needles, *or size to obtain gauge*

Yarn needle

GAUGE
20 sts and 32 rows = 4"/10cm in Stockinette Stitch (knit every round)

Always take time to check your gauge.

20%
of "sock people" polled admit to having a major sock fetish— the first step toward recovery.

ANKLE
Change to C.

Round 1: Knit.

Rounds 2–16: Work in K2, p2 Rib for 15 rounds.

Note: Each time the color is changed, work the indicated number of rounds by knitting the first round and working in the established rib pattern for the remaining number of rounds.

Change to A, and continue as established for 8 rounds.

Change to B, and continue as established for 8 rounds.

CALF
Change to C.

Next round: Knit.

Next round: Work in K2, p2 Rib.

Next round (increase round): *(Kfb in next st) twice, p2; repeat from * around—60 (72) sts.

Next round: *K4, p2; repeat from * around.

Repeat last round 4 more times.

Change to B, and continue as established for 12 (20) rounds.

Change to A, and continue as established for 12 rounds.

Change to C, and continue as established for 8 rounds.

Change to A, and continue as established for 12 rounds.

Change to B, and continue as established for 12 rounds.

Change to C, and continue as established for 8 rounds.

Change to C, and continue as established for 28 rounds.

Bind off loosely in K2, p2 Rib.

LEG #2

Work as for leg #1 to ankle.

ANKLE

Change to A.

Round 1: Knit.

Rounds 2–24: Work in K2, p2 Rib for 23 rounds.

Change to C, and continue as established for 8 rounds.

CALF

Change to B.

Next round: Knit.

Next round: Work in K2, p2 Rib.

Next round (increase round): *(Kfb in next st) twice, p2; repeat from * around—60 (72) sts.

Next round: *K4, p2; repeat from * around.

Repeat last round 4 (12) more times.

Change to A, and continue as established for 8 rounds.

Change to C, and continue as established for 24 rounds.

Change to B, and continue as established for 8 rounds.

Change to A, and continue as established for 8 rounds.

KNEE AND LOWER THIGH

Continue with C.

Next round: Knit.

Next round: Work in K2, p2 Rib.

Repeat last round 14 more times.

Change to A, and continue as established for 20 (28) rounds.

Change to C, and continue as established for 8 rounds.

Change to A, and continue as established for 8 rounds.

KNEE AND LOWER THIGH

Continue with C.

Next round: Knit.

Next round: Work in K2, p2 Rib.

Repeat last round 10 more times.

Change to B, and continue as established for 16 (24) rounds.

Change to C, and continue as established for 20 rounds.

Change to A, and continue as established for 16 rounds.

Bind off loosely in K2, p2 Rib.

FINISHING

Weave in ends. With D, sew a few stitches on either side of each heel opening to reinforce. Block if desired.

This project was knit with:

Blue Sky Alpaca's Sport, sport weight, 100% alpaca, 1.75oz/50g = approx 110yd/99m per skein
(A) 2 skeins, #509 natural dark gray
(B) 2 skeins, #508 natural medium gray
(C) 2 skeins, #507 natural light gray
(D) 1 skein, #511 red

SKILL LEVEL
Intermediate

FINISHED MEASUREMENTS
Foot circumference 8"/20.5cm

Leg length 10"/25.5cm

Foot length 8½ (9½+)"/21.5 (24+)cm

MATERIALS AND TOOLS
Approx total: 400yd/360m of
(1) fingering weight yarn,
superwash wool/tencel
blend, in blue/purple variegated

Knitting needles: 2.5mm
(size 1½ U.S.) set of 5
double-pointed needles,
or size to obtain gauge

Stitch markers (optional)

Stitch holder

Yarn needle

GAUGE
32 sts and 42 rows = 4"/10cm
in Stockinette Stitch (knit
every round)

*Always take time to check your
gauge.*

Rock-A-Bye

Need to reconnect? A little porch sitting and
stellar diagonal-ribbed socks—of course—
are just what the doctor ordered.

by GINA HOUSE

CUFF

Cast on 64 sts onto one needle. Distribute the stitches evenly over four needles (16 sts per needle). Place a stitch marker for beginning of round. Taking care not to twist stitches, join to work in the round.

Work in K1, p1 Ribbing pattern for 1"/2.5cm.

LEFT SOCK

Work 32 rounds in Modified Diagonal Rib #1 pattern.

Work 32 rounds in Modified Diagonal Rib #2 pattern. End ready to work across stitches on needle #4.

HEEL FLAP

Redistribute stitches as follows: Slip the 32 stitches from needles #1 and #4 onto a single needle and knit back and forth over these stitches only (for heel). The remaining 32 stitches on needles #2 and #3 are held (for instep).

Row 1 (RS): Sl 1, k3, p4, (k4, p4) 3 times.

Row 2 (WS): Repeat row 1.

Repeat last 2 rows 15 more times or until heel flap measures approx 3"/7.5cm.

Turn Heel

Continue to work back and forth on heel stitches only.

Row 1 (RS): Sl 1, k17, ssk, k1, turn.

Row 2 (WS): Sl 1, p5, p2tog, p1, turn.

Row 3: Sl 1, k6, ssk, k1, turn.

Row 4: Sl 1, p7, p2tog, p1, turn.

Continue working in this manner working one additional stitch before the decrease on each row, until 18 stitches remain, ending with a WS row.

Note: On the last two rows, there will be no extra stitch to work after the decrease.

Pick-up round: With RS of heel facing and spare needle, sl 1, k8 heel sts; with another needle, k9 remaining heel sts, pick up and k18 sts along side of heel flap, pick up and k1 st in the corner (needle #1); work row 1 of Modified Diagonal Rib #1 pattern across held instep stitches (needles #2 and #3); with another needle, pick up and k1 st in the corner, pick up and k18 sts along the opposite side of heel flap, k sts from spare needle (needle #4)—88 sts (28 sts each on needles #1 and #4, and 32 sts on needles #2 and #3).

Shape Gusset
Round 1:

Needle #1: Knit to last 3 sts, k2tog, k1—27 sts;

Needles #2 and #3: Continue in established Modified Diagonal Rib #1 pattern—32 sts;

Needle #4: K1, ssk, knit to end—27 sts.

Round 2:

Needle #1: Knit;

Needles #2 and #3: Continue in established Modified Diagonal Rib #1 pattern;

Needle #4: Knit.

Repeat last 2 rounds until 64 stitches remain (32 instep stitches, and 32 heel stitches).

FOOT

Continue in Modified Diagonal Rib #1 as established.

Note: This pattern will be repeated twice for both sizes from gusset down the leg.

Round 1:

Needle #1: Knit;

Needles #2 and #3: Continue in established Modified Diagonal Rib #1 pattern;

Needle #4: Knit.

Repeat last round until 32 rounds (total) of Modified Diagonal Rib #1 pattern have been worked from gusset, and 16 rounds of Modified Diagonal Rib #2 pattern have been worked.

Next 2 rounds:

Needle #1: Knit;

Needles #2 and #3: (K4, p4) 3 times, knit to end;

Needle #4: Knit.

Next 2 rounds:

Needle #1: Knit;

Needles #2 and #3: (K4, p4) 2 times, knit to end;

Needle #4: Knit.

Next 2 rounds:

Needle #1: Knit;

Needles #2 and #3: (K4, p4), knit to end;

Needle #4: Knit.

Next 2 rounds: Knit.

For larger size only: Knit rounds until foot measures approx 2"/5cm less than desired foot length.

End ready to work stitches from needle #1.

modified diagonal rib #1 (multiples of 8)

Rounds 1 and 2: *K4, p4; repeat from * around.
Rounds 3 and 4: P1, k4, *p4, k4; repeat from * to last 3 sts, p3.
Rounds 5 and 6: P2, k4, *p4, k4; repeat from * to last 2 sts, p2.
Rounds 7 and 8: P3, k4, *p4, k4; repeat from * to last st, p1.
Rounds 9 and 10: *P4, k4; repeat from * around.
Rounds 11 and 12: K1, *p4, k4; repeat from * to last 3 sts, k3.
Rounds 13 and 14: K2, *p4, k4; repeat from * to last 2 sts, k2.
Rounds 15 and 16: K3, *p4, k4; repeat from * to last st, k1.
Repeat rounds 1–16 for Modified Diagonal Rib #1 pattern.

modified diagonal rib #2 (multiples of 8)

Rounds 1 and 2: *K4, p4; repeat from * around.
Rounds 3 and 4: K3, *p4, k4; repeat from * to last st, k1.
Rounds 5 and 6: K2, *p4, k4; repeat from * to last 2 sts, k2.
Rounds 7 and 8: K1, *p4, k4; repeat from * to last 3 sts, k3.
Rounds 9 and 10: *P4, k4; repeat from * around.
Rounds 11 and 12: P3, k4, *p4, k4; repeat from * to last st, p1.
Rounds 13 and 14: P2, k4, *p4, k4; repeat from * to last 2 sts, p2.
Rounds 15 and 16: P1, k4, *p4, k4; repeat from * to last 3 sts, p3.
Repeat rounds 1–16 for Modified Diagonal Rib #2 pattern.

SOCKTALK GINA HOUSE on....favorite positions

Positions, positions…one of my favorite topics. There are so many places that socks can be knit with delicious pleasure. My all-time favorite position is standing by the kitchen counter in summer, with little in my hands but a flimsy pair of needles and a lace weight, angora-blend yarn. Oh, that yarn is hot! The socks you knit with this combination are liable to make you pant like a dog. Whew…I can almost feel the heat now!

Shape Toe
Round 1:

Needle #1: Knit to last 3 sts, k2tog, k1;

Needle #2: K1, ssk, knit to end;

Needle #3: Knit to last 3 sts, k2tog, k1;

Needle #4: K1, ssk, knit to end.

Round 2: Knit.

Repeat last two rounds until 24 total stitches remain. End with round 2.

Finish Toe
Cut yarn, leaving a 30"/76cm tail. Use Kitchener Stitch to sew the two sets of stitches together.

RIGHT SOCK
Work 32 rounds in Modified Diagonal Rib #2 pattern.

Work 32 rounds in Modified Diagonal Rib #1 pattern. End ready to work across stitches on needle #4.

HEEL FLAP AND TURN HEEL
Work heel flap and turn heel as for left sock.

Pick-up round: With RS of heel facing and spare needle, sl 1, k8 heel sts; with another needle, k9 remaining heel sts, pick up and k18 sts along side of heel flap, pick up and k1 st in the corner (needle #1); work row 1 of Modified Diagonal Rib #2 pattern across held instep stitches (needles #2 and #3); with another needle, pick up and k1 st in the corner, pick up and k18 sts along the opposite side of heel flap, k sts from spare needle (needle #4)—88 sts (28 sts each on needles #1 and #4, and 32 sts on needles #2 and #3).

off the charts

modified diagonal rib #1

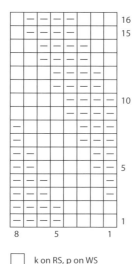

modified diagonal rib #2

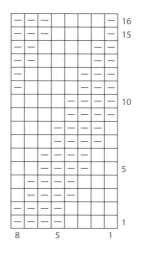

☐ k on RS, p on WS

— p on RS, k on WS

Shape Gusset

Round 1:

Needle #1: Knit to last 3 sts, k2tog, k1—27 sts;

Needles #2 and #3: Continue in established Modified Diagonal Rib #2 pattern—32 sts;

Needle #4: K1, ssk, knit to end—27 sts.

Round 2:

Needle #1: Knit;

Needles #2 and #3: Continue in established Modified Diagonal Rib #2 pattern;

Needle #4: Knit.

Repeat last 2 rounds until 64 stitches remain (32 instep stitches, and 32 heel stitches).

FOOT

Continue in Modified Diagonal Rib #2 as established.

Note: This pattern will be repeated twice for both sizes from gusset down the leg.

Round 1:

Needle #1: Knit;

Needles #2 and #3: Continue in established Modified

Diagonal Rib #2 pattern;

Needle #4: Knit.

Repeat last round until 32 rounds (total) of Modified Diagonal Rib #2 pattern have been worked from gusset, and 16 rounds of Modified Diagonal Rib #1 pattern have been worked.

Next 2 rounds:

Needle #1: Knit;

Needles #2 and #3: K8, (k4, p4) 3 times;

Needle #4: Knit.

Next 2 rounds:

Needle #1: Knit;

Needles #2 and #3: K16, (k4, p4) 2 times;

Needle #4: Knit.

Next 2 rounds:

Needle #1: Knit;

Needles #2 and #3: K24, (k4, p4);

Needle #4: Knit.

Next 2 rounds: Knit.

For larger size only: Knit rounds until foot measures ap-

prox 2"/5cm less than desired foot length.

End ready to work stitches from needle #1.

Shape toe and finish as for left sck.

FINISHING

Weave in ends.

Tip: A larger circumference sock can be made following these same instructions by using a larger needle size or using sport weight yarn instead of fingering weight.

This project was knit with:

Sereknity SockOptions' Satin Sock, fingering weight, 50% superwash merino, 50% tencel, 3.75oz/106g = approx 400yd/360m per skein 1 skein, Blue Hawaii colorway

SKILL LEVEL
Intermediate

FINISHED MEASUREMENTS
Foot circumference
8"/20.5cm

Leg length 7"/18cm

Foot length 8"/20.5cm

MATERIALS AND TOOLS
Approx total: 175yd/158m of
🧶1️⃣ fingering weight yarn,
wool/silk/nylon blend, in
pink

Knitting needles: 2mm
(size 0 U.S.) set of 5
double-pointed needles, *or
size to obtain gauge*

Stitch marker (optional)

Yarn needle

GAUGE
36 sts and 48 rows = 4"/10cm
in Stockinette Stitch (knit
every round)

*Always take time to check
your gauge.*

Special Abbreviations
Make bobble (mb): (k1, p1,
k1, p1, k1) into st to make
5 sts, turn, p5, turn, pass
sts 2, 3, 4, and 5 over first
st one at a time, then k into
back of this st.

Movie Socks

Three things that make our mouths water:
movies with Johnny Depp, the smell of
hot buttery popcorn, and these pretty
anklet socks—delicate but with a certain
touch-me quality.

by KATE BLACKBURN

CUFF

Cast on 72 sts onto one needle. Distribute the stitches evenly over four needles (18 sts per needle). Place a stitch marker for beginning of round. Taking care not to twist stitches, join to work in the round.

Rounds 1–8: Knit.

Round 9 (fold line): *Yo, k2tog; repeat from * around.

Rounds 10–18: Knit.

Round 19 (join cast-on edge to inside of sock): Fold cast-on edge inward along fold line (round 9); knit around inserting needle into st on the needle and through one of the cast-on loops for each st.

Round 20: Knit.

LEG

Work Bobble and Lace Stitch pattern 3 times (48 rounds total), or desired number of complete pattern repeats.

HEEL FLAP

Next row: K18, turn.

Next row: Sl 1, p35, turn.

You should now have 36 heel flap stitches, with the remaining 36 stitches held on two needles for the instep.

Row 1 (RS): *Sl 1, k35.

Row 2: Sl 1, p35.

Repeat last 2 rows for a total of 34 rows, ending with a WS row.

Turn Heel

Row 1 (RS): Sl 1, k19, ssk, k1, turn.

Row 2: Sl 1, p5, p2tog, p1, turn.

Row 3: Sl 1, k6, ssk, k1, turn.

Row 4: Sl 1, p7, p2tog, p1, turn.

Continue working in this manner, working one additional stitch before the decrease on each row, until 20 stitches remain, ending with a WS row.

Note: On the last two rows, there will be no extra stitch to work after the decrease.

Pick-up round: With RS of heel facing, knit across the 20 heel flap sts; with another needle, pick up 18 sts along side of heel flap, and pick up 2 additional sts at the corner (needle #1); with two more needles, work row 1 of Lace Stitch across 36 instep sts (needles #2 and #3—18 sts on each); with another needle, pick up 2 sts in the corner, pick up 18 sts along the opposite side of heel flap, then knit across 10 sts of the heel flap (needle #4); slip remaining 10 sts of heel flap onto the end of needle #1. You should now have 30 sts on needle #1, 18 sts on needles #2 and #3, and 30 sts on needle #4—96 sts (total).

Next round (twist picked-up sts and close holes at corners):

Needle #1: K10, K18 tbl, ssk—29 sts;

Needles #2 and #3: Work row 2 of Lace Stitch pattern;

Needle #4: K2tog, k18 tbl, k10—29 sts.

bobble and lace stitch (multiples of 18 sts)

Round 1: Yo, k1, [yo, ssk] twice, yo, k2, ssk, k5, k2tog, k2.
Rounds 2, 4, 6, 8, 10, 12, 14, and 16: Knit.
Round 3: Yo, k3, [yo, ssk] twice, yo, k2, ssk, k3, k2tog, k2.
Round 5: Yo, k2, mb, k2, [yo, ssk] twice, yo, k2, ssk, k1, k2tog, k2.
Round 7: Yo, k2, mb, k1, mb, k2, [yo, ssk] twice, yo, k2, skp, k2.
Round 9: Ssk, k5, k2tog, k2, [yo, k2tog] twice, yo, k1, yo, k2.
Round 11: Ssk, k3, k2tog, k2, [yo, k2tog] twice, yo, k3, yo, k2.
Round 13: Ssk, k1, k2tog, k2, [yo, k2tog] twice, yo, k2, mb, k2, yo, k2.
Round 15: Skp, k2, [yo, k2tog] twice, yo, k2, mb, k1, mb, k2, yo, k2.
Repeat rounds 1–16 for Bobble and Lace Stitch pattern.

lace stitch (multiples of 18 sts)

Row 1: Yo, k1, [yo, ssk] twice, yo, k2, ssk, k5, k2tog, k2.
Rows 2, 4, 6, 8, 10, 12, 14, and 16: Knit.
Row 3: Yo, k3, [yo, ssk] twice, yo, k2, ssk, k3, k2tog, k2.
Row 5: Yo, k5, [yo, ssk] twice, yo, k2, ssk, k1, k2tog, k2.
Row 7: Yo, k7, [yo, ssk] twice, yo, k2, skp, k2.
Row 9: Ssk, k5, k2tog, k2, [yo, k2tog] twice, yo, k1, yo, k2.
Row 11: Ssk, k3, k2tog, k2, [yo, k2tog] twice, yo, k3, yo, k2.
Row 13: Ssk, k1, k2tog, k2, [yo, k2tog] twice, yo, k5, yo, k2.
Row 15: Skp, k2, [yo, k2tog] twice, yo, k7, yo, k2.
Repeat rows 1–16 for Lace Stitch pattern.

GUSSET
Round 1:

Needle #1: Knit to last 3 sts, k2tog, k1—28 sts;

Needles #2 and #3: Continue in Lace Stitch pattern as established;

Needle #4: K1, ssk, k to end—28 sts.

Round 2:

Needles #1 and #4: Knit to end;

Needles #2 and #3: Continue in Lace Stitch pattern as established.

Repeat rounds 1 and 2 until there are 18 sts remaining on needles #1 and #4—72 sts (total).

Work rounds in established pattern, without further decreasing until foot measures 7½"/19cm, or 1½"/4cm less than desired total foot length; end after an even-numbered round (even-numbered row of Lace Stitch pattern).

Shape Toe
Round 1: Knit.

Round 2:

Needles #1 and #3: Knit to last 3 sts, k2tog, k1;

Needles #2 and #4: K1, ssk, k to end—68 sts (total).

Repeat rounds 1 and 2 eight more times—36 sts remain.

Finish Toe

Next round: Knit sts of needle #1 onto needle #4; slip sts of needle #2 onto needle #3, so there are now two needles with 18 sts on each. Cut yarn, leaving a 20"/51cm tail. Use Kitchener Stitch to sew the two sets of stitches together.

FINISHING

Weave in ends.

This project was knit with:

**Regia's 4-ply Silk, fingering weight, 55% new wool, 25% nylon, 20% silk, 1.75oz/50g = approx 219yd/197m per ball
1 ball, #035 rose**

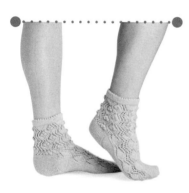

off the charts

bobble and lace stitch

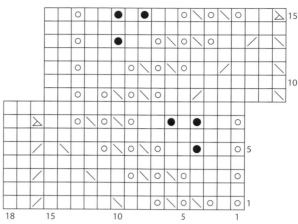

lace stitch

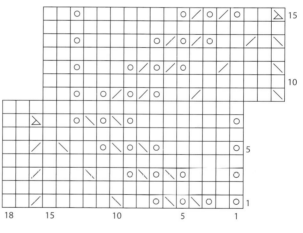

	k on RS, p on WS
○	yarn over
╱	k2tog
╲	ssk
⋋	skp
●	(k1, p1, k1, p1, k1) st to make 5 sts, turn, p5, turn, pass sts 2, 3, 4, and 5 over first st one time, then k into back of this st.

47

Why is it that when it comes to shirts and socks, "borrowed" ones from your guy just feel so comfy? A veritable Fair Isle love-fest, these are as cozy as they are cute.

Boyfriend Socks

by MARY JANE MUCKLESTONE

94% of sock knitters said their favorite sock yarn is wool.

SKILL LEVEL
Experienced

FINISHED MEASUREMENTS
Foot circumference 10"/25.5cm

Leg length 9½"/24cm

Foot length 9"/23cm

MATERIALS AND TOOLS
Approx total: 444yd/400m of (3) DK weight yarn, wool

Color A: 200yd/180m of (3) DK weight yarn, wool, in dark green

Color B: 42yd/38m of (3) DK weight yarn, wool, in pale yellow

Color C: 38yd/34m of (3) DK weight yarn, wool, in green

Color D: 38yd/34m of (3) DK weight yarn, wool, in yellow

Color E: 50yd/45m of (3) DK weight yarn, wool, in rust

Color F: 50yd/45m of (3) DK weight yarn, wool, in dark yellow

Color G: 13yd/12m of (3) DK weight yarn, wool, in dark brown

Color H: 13yd/12m of (3) DK weight yarn, wool, in light blue

Knitting needles: 2.75mm (size 2 U.S.) and 3.25mm (size 3 U.S.) sets of 5 double-pointed needles, *or size to obtain gauge*

Waste yarn—approx 1yd/1m (for holding heel stitches)

Yarn needle

GAUGE
29 sts and 29 rows = 4"/10cm over Fair Isle pattern in Stockinette Stitch (knit every round)

Always take time to check your gauge.

Note: This sock pattern includes instructions for designated Right and Left sock.

RIGHT SOCK

CUFF
With smaller needles, cast on 72 sts. Distribute the stitches evenly over three needles (24 sts per needle). Taking care not to twist stitches, join to work in the round.

Round 1: *K1, p1; repeat from * around.

Repeat round 1 until piece measures 1"/2.5cm from beginning.

LEG
Change to larger needles and work Chart A, changing colors as indicated, and repeating 18 sts of each row 4 times.

HEEL
Set Up: With waste yarn, knit 36 sts. Cut waste yarn. Slide stitches back to the beginning of the round (where the waste yarn begins).

Work Chart B, changing colors as indicated, and repeating 24 sts of each row 3 times.

Shape Toe
Carefully redistribute the stitches over four needles. Beginning at seam, place 18 stitches on each needle.

Round 1: *K1, ssk, K30, k2tog, k1; repeat from * once more—68 sts.

Round 2: Knit.

Repeat rounds 1 and 2 four more times (there will be one fewer stitch on each needle after every decrease round)—52 sts.

Repeat round 1 until 4 sts remain on each needle—16 sts total.

Finish Toe
Place the eight back stitches together on one needle, place the eight front stitches together on another needle. Cut the yarn leaving a 10"/25.5cm tail. Use Kitchener Stitch to sew the two sets of eight stitches together.

Shape Heel
Carefully pull out the waste yarn knit into half of the stitches at the point between Chart A and Chart B. There should be 36 live stitches on one edge and 35 live stitches on the other edge. Place these stitches on four needles beginning at the side where the seam runs down the left leg and working around the opening. Place 18 stitches on each of three needles and 17 stitches on the fourth needle.

Pick-Up and Knit Heel Stitches: With one needle and A, pick up and knit the strand between sts (between the edges of the waste yarn opening), knit the first 18 sts (needle #1); with another needle, knit the next 18 sts (needle #2); with another empty needle, pick up and knit the strand between sts (between the edges of the waste yarn opening), knit the next 18 sts (needle #3); with another empty needle, knit the last 17 sts, then pick up and knit the strand between sts (needle #4)—74 sts (19 sts on needle #1, 18 sts on needle #2, 19 sts on needle #3, and 18 sts on needle #4).

Rounds 1–4: Knit.

Round 5: [K1, ssk, k each remaining st on needle; k each st on next needle to last 3 sts on needle, k2tog, k1] 2 times—70 sts.

chart a

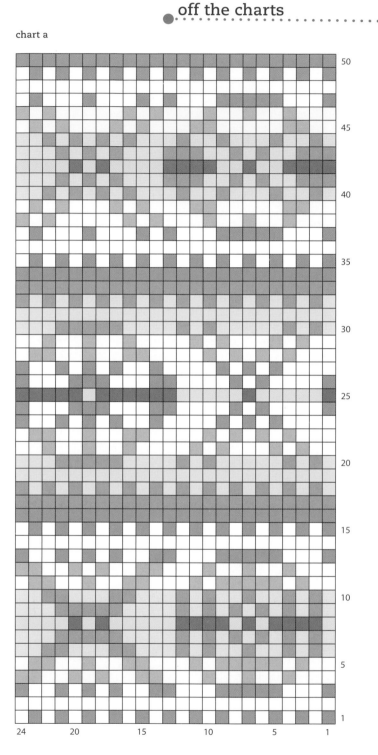

Repeat last round until 14 stitches remain (4 sts on needle #1, 3 sts on needle #2, 4 sts on needle #3, and 3 sts on needle #4).

Finish Heel

Knit across the stitches of needle #2 with needle #1. Knit across the stitches of needle #4 with needle #3. Cut the yarn, leaving a 10"/25.5cm tail. Use Kitchener Stitch to sew the two sets of seven stitches together.

LEFT SOCK

Work as for Right Sock, through completion of Chart A. After completing Chart A, set up heel as follows:

Heel Set Up: Slip the last 36 sts of the round backwards. With waste yarn, knit into these 36 sts. Cut waste yarn. Slide stitches back to the beginning of the round (where the waste yarn begins).

Complete as for Right Sock except place seam so that it runs down the right side of the leg when picking-up and knitting the heel stitches.

chart b

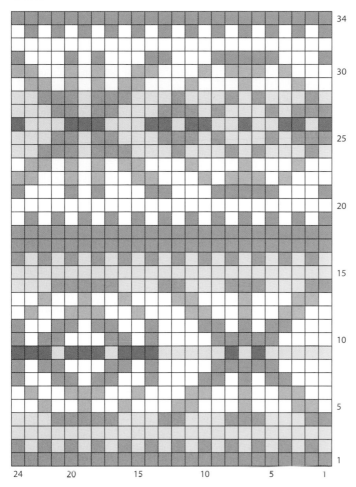

24   20   15   10   5   1

34
30
25
20
15
10
5
1

FINISHING

Weave in ends. Lightly block socks, if desired.

Tip: You may want to use reinforcing yarn along with the wool in the heels and toes.

This project was knit with:

Jamieson & Smith's 2-ply Jumper Weight, DK weight, 100% Shetland wool, 1oz/28.5g = approx 150yd/135m per skein
(A) 2 skeins, #82 dark green (approx 200yd/183m)
(B) 1 skein, #FC43 pale yellow (approx 42yd/39m)
(C) 1 skein, #118 green (approx 38yd/35m)
(D) 1 skein, #121 yellow (approx 38yd/35m)
(E) 1 skein, #122 rust (approx 50yd/46m)
(F) 1 skein, #28 dark yellow (approx 50yd/46m)
(G) 1 skein, #5 dark brown (approx 13yd/12m)
(H) 1 skein, #14 light blue (approx 13yd/12m)

- (A) dark green
- (B) pale yellow
- (C) green
- (D) yellow
- (E) rust
- (F) dark yellow
- (G) dark brown
- (H) light blue

SKILL LEVEL
Intermediate

FINISHED MEASUREMENTS
Foot circumference 9"/23cm

Leg length 6¼"/16cm

Foot length 9½"/24cm

MATERIALS AND TOOLS
Approx total: 480yd/432m of ⑪ fingering weight yarn, wool/bamboo blend

    Color A: 96yd/86m of ⑪ fingering weight yarn, wool/bamboo blend, in light purple

    Color B: 48yd/43m of ⑪ fingering weight yarn, wool/bamboo blend, in pale green

    Color C: 96yd/86m of ⑪ fingering weight yarn, wool/bamboo blend, in violet/blue/green variegated

    Color D: 96yd/86m of ⑪ fingering weight yarn, wool/bamboo blend, in green/orange variegated

    Color E: 48yd/43m of ⑪ fingering weight yarn, wool/bamboo blend, in teal/ultramarine variegated

    Color F: 48yd/43m of ⑪ fingering weight yarn, wool/bamboo blend, in pink

    Color G: 48yd/43m of ⑪ fingering weight yarn, wool/bamboo blend, in orange

Knitting needles: 3.25mm (size 3 U.S.) set of 4 double-pointed needles, and 3.5mm (size 4 U.S.) set of 4 double-pointed needles, *or size to obtain gauge*

Stitch marker

Stitch holder

Yarn needle or crochet hook

GAUGE
32 sts and 10 rows = 4"/10cm in Stockinette Stitch (knit every round)

Always take time to check your gauge.

Note: Twining can cause constriction of your work. It is recommended that you endeavor to twine loosely, but use one size larger needles than you are accustomed to, so that the socks will fit.

Special Instructions for Twined Knitting
With two different strands of yarn (both held in same hand if possible) work as follows: K1 with A, drop A; k1 with B bringing B up and across A, drop B; k1 with A, bringing A up and across B. Each stitch is formed by having the two yarns "twine" or cross. If done properly, this results in knitting that appears "normal" on the front; however, the back appears to be "braided" as the colors cross. The resulting fabric is stretchy and flexible, yet warm. This method is well over 400 years old. When only one color is specified, do not try to "twine."

Breakfast in Bed

Seems like everything is tastier when it's served to you in bed.
For your dining pleasure, try this pair of twined socks,
complete with a lovebird pattern.

by LAURA ANDERSSON

RUFFLE CUFF

With smaller needles and A, cast on 144 sts. Distribute sts evenly over three needles (48 sts per needle). Place a stitch marker for beginning of round. Taking care not to twist sts, join to work in the round. Purl 1 round.

Decrease round: *P2tog; repeat from * around—72 sts.

Knit 1 round.

Note: If no ruffle is desired, cast on 72 sts and join to work in the round. Purl 2 rounds, knit 1 round.

Corrugated Rib

Note: Corrugated Rib is a common element of Fair Isle knitting. It consists of a "faux" ribbing where the knit stitches are worked with one color and the purl stitches are worked with another color. The colors change often, echoing colors that will be used in the garment. Corrugated ribbing is called "faux ribbing" because the color change destroys the normal elasticity of ribbing.

Round 1: Join B and knit 1 round.

Next 5 rounds: *K2 with A, p2 with B; repeat from * around. Cut B. Join C.

Next 3 rounds: *K2 with A, p2 with C; repeat from * around. Cut A. Join D.

Next 5 rounds: *K2 with C, p2 with D; repeat from * around. Cut D. Join E.

Next 3 rounds: *K2 with C, p2 with E; repeat from * around. Cut C.

LEG

Round 1: Join B, *kfb, k23; repeat from * around—75 sts.

Change to larger needles.

Work all rounds of chart 1.

Work all rounds of chart 2.

Note: The three rounds that make up the flower center are critical in terms of fit! Consider working very, very loosely, and/or going up 1 or 2 needle sizes for these rounds to avoid disaster. This is because there are only two colors used in a repeat of 15 stitches, so it's easy to tighten unintentionally.

Alternatively, work these rounds using intarsia or duplicate stitch, with a new strand of color for just the flower centers.

HEEL

Set up for heel, as follows: Beginning at center back marker, kfb, k18, turn. Cut F and join D and G.

Begin twined heel: [P1 with D, p1 with G] 20 times, turn—40 sts.

The heel is worked entirely with D and G. These colors are also used for the gusset pick ups and the first instep round. Place remaining 36 sts on a stitch holder or waste yarn (for instep).

Notes:

1. You will not slip the first stitch on either side of heel flap.

2. You will alternate every stitch with a different color throughout (twining).

Next row (RS): *K1 with G, k1 with D; repeat from * across.

Next row (WS): *P1 with G, p1 with D; repeat from * across.

Repeat last 2 rows until heel measures approx 2¾"/7cm. End with a WS row.

Turn Heel

Note: If you wish, you can simplify turning the heel as follows: cut G and work the heel turn and first gusset round with D only.

Row 1 (RS): [K1 with G, k1 with D] 11 times, k2tog, k1, turn—15 sts unworked.

Note: Ignore the color of the unworked sts on right needle. Focus only on the left needle to alternate as you work.

Row 2 (WS): [P1 with G, p1 with D] 3 times, p2tog, p1—15 sts unworked.

Row 3: *K1 with G, k1 with D; repeat from * to 1 st before gap, k2tog, k1, turn—13 sts unworked.

Row 4: *P1 with G, p1 with D; repeat from * to 1 st before gap, k2tog, k1, turn—13 sts unworked.

Repeat last 2 rows until all sts have been consumed, and you have 22 stitches. End with a WS row.

Note: On the last two rows, there will be no extra stitch to work after the decrease.

GUSSET

Continue alternating G and D throughout.

Pick-up round: With RS of heel facing, knit the first 11 sts of the heel onto a needle and set it aside (needle #3); knit across the remaining 11 heel sts, (look at last st on needle, and pick up using that color only) pick up and knit 18 sts along side of heel flap (needle #1); knit across held sts (needle #2); (pick up using the color you did NOT use on the opposite side of heel flap) pick up and knit 18 sts along opposite side of heel flap and

off the charts

chart 1

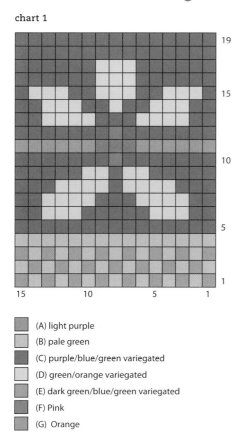

chart 2

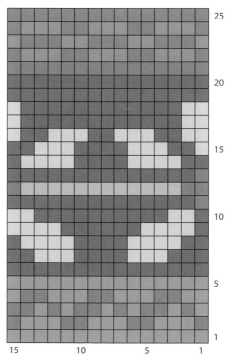

(A) light purple

(B) pale green

(C) purple/blue/green variegated

(D) green/orange variegated

(E) dark green/blue/green variegated

(F) Pink

(G) Orange

knit across stitches held on needle #3—94 sts (29 sts each on needles #1 and #2, 36 sts on needle #3).

Note: If you wish, you can simplify turning the pick-up round as follows: Cut G and work the pick-up round with D only.

Cut D and G. Join A.

Gusset Decreases
Decrease round:

Needle #1: Knit to last 3 sts, k2tog, k1—28 sts;

Needle #2: Knit to end;

Needle #3: K1, skp, knit to end—35 sts.

Next round: Knit.

Note: If you wish, work the plain Stockinette rounds using the smaller needles.

Repeat last 2 rounds, and AT THE SAME TIME:

1. Work 1 more round with A only.

2. Work 3 rounds alternating A and E. **Note: The last stitch on needle #1 and first stitch on needle #3 are not in pattern, but are always knit with E.**

3. Work all rows of LoveBirds chart across instep stitches, as follows:

Work first 2 rounds of chart with E only, then join F.

Needle #1: Work in twined checks, alternating E and F (except the stitch closest to the instep. Keep this stitch in the same color during all rows);

Needle #2: Work Love Birds chart;

Needle #3: Work in twined checks alternating E and F.

Continue working chart as established until stitch count has been reduced to 72 sts. Then continue even as established until chart is completed.

Continue with no further decreases as follows:

Next 3 rounds: Work in twined checks alternating D and E.

Next 2 rounds: Knit with D only.

Next 2 rounds: Work in twined checks alternating D and C.

Shape Toe
Decrease round:

Needle #1: *K2 with D, k2 with C; repeat from * to last 3 sts, maintain twined checks, k2tog, k1;

Needle #2: Maintain twined double-checks as established, k1, skp, continue in pattern to last 3 sts, k2tog, k1;

Needle #3: Maintain twined double-checks as established, k1, skp, continue in pattern to end.

Next round: Continue in twined check pattern.

Repeat last 2 rounds, swapping location of colors D and C.

Next round:

Needle #1: *K1 with D, k1 with C; repeat from * to last 3 sts, maintain twined checks, k2tog, k1;

Needle #2: Maintain twined checks, k1, skp, continue in pattern to last 3 sts, k2tog, k1;

Needle #3: Maintain twined checks, k1, skp, continue in pattern to end. Cut D.

Next round: With C, knit.

Repeat last 2 rounds, and AT THE SAME TIME:

1. Work 1 more round with C only.

2. Work 2 rounds alternating C and B. Cut C.

3. Work 1 round with B only.

4. Work 1 round alternating G and B. Cut B.

5. Work 1 round with G only.

6. Work 2 rounds alternating A and G.

7. Work 2 rounds with A only. Cut G.

8. Work rounds alternating A and F, until only 8 stitches remain.

Cut yarn and thread tail through remaining stitches. Pull tight and secure on WS of sock.

FINISHING
Turn sock inside out and weave in ends with a crochet hook or yarn needle. It is best to work a specific color end into its own color. Patience is well worth it! It is recommended that you work an end into at least 3 stitches up and back (to ensure that your work doesn't unravel). Block if desired.

lovebirds

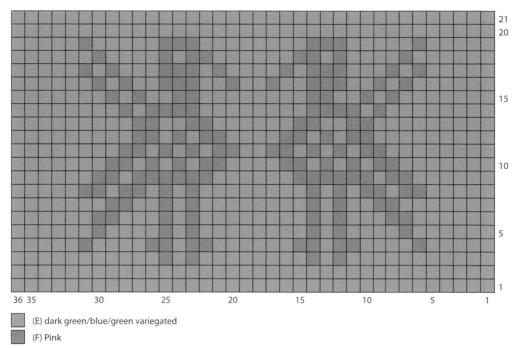

▨	(E) dark green/blue/green variegated	
▨	(F) Pink	

This project was knit with:

Crystal Palace Yarn's
Panda Superwash, finger-
ing weight, 46% bamboo,
43% superwash wool, 11 %
nylon, 1.75oz/50g = approx
170yd/153m per ball
(A) 1 ball, #9628 periwinkle
(B) 1 ball, #2304 misty green
(C) 1 ball, #9812 violets
(D) 1 ball, #0443 basil curry
(E) 1 ball, #9573 ultramarine
(F) 1 ball, #2013 magenta
(G) 1 ball, #4105 mandarin
orange

SOCKTALK LAURA ANDERSSON on... favorite knitting spots

" I've found that I can knit while I'm dozing off… and keep knitting in my sleep. Sometimes it means that I have to check the
count the next day, but it's usually okay for ribbing. "

Quickie Socks

Knitted socks are a labor of love, but we say less labor, more lovin'! Knit with worsted weight yarn, these socks work up quick with an easy-to-memorize offset rib pattern.

by SUSAN PIERCE LAWRENCE

SKILL LEVEL
Intermediate

FINISHED MEASUREMENTS
Foot circumference 6"/15cm

Leg length 5½"/14cm

Foot length 8½"/21.5cm

Note: This sock is very stretchy and will fit a wide range of foot circumferences.

MATERIALS AND TOOLS
Approx total: 200yd/180m of **(4)** worsted weight yarn, wool, in gray

Knitting needles: 3.75mm (size 5 U.S.) set of 5 double-pointed needles, *or size to obtain gauge*

Stitch marker (optional)

Waste yarn

Yarn needle

GAUGE
28 sts and 28 rows = 4"/10cm in Stockinette Stitch (knit every round)

Always take time to check your gauge.

rib & garter stitch (multiples of 2 sts)

Rounds 1, 8, 10, and 17: Knit.
Rounds 2–7: *K1, p1; repeat from * around.
Rounds 9 and 18: Purl.
Rounds 11–16: *P1, k1; repeat from * around.
Repeat rounds 1–18 for Rib & Garter Stitch pattern.

CUFF

Loosely cast on 40 sts onto one needle. Distribute the stitches evenly over four needles (10 sts per needle). Place a stitch marker for beginning of round. Taking care not to twist stitches, join to work in the round so the purl side of the cast-on edge is on the RS.

Rounds 1, 3, and 5: Knit.

Rounds 2, 4, and 6: Purl.

LEG

Work Rib and Garter Stitch pattern 2 times (36 rounds total). The leg of the sock should measure approximately 5½"/14cm from the cast-on edge.

HEEL FLAP

Set-Up: K21, place the next 19 sts onto a piece of waste yarn. Turn work so the WS is facing you. Work back and forth over the 21 heel flap stitches only.

Rows 1, 3, and 5: Sl 1, k19, p1, turn.

Rows 2 and 4: Sl 1, k20, turn.

The Sock Curse

Ladies, beware! Old wives say to never knit a man socks, because if you do, he'll walk away from you, but who says that's a bad thing? If you do knit him socks early on in the relationship and he leaves you, you won't regret wasting so much time with an ungrateful man. You'll also have more time to knit socks for yourself, your loving family, and your co-workers, the people that appreciate you and all your hard work. The sock curse, depending on how you look at it, might not be a curse at all; it might be a blessing.

Shape Heel
Short-Row Decreases

Row 1 (RS): Sl 1, k19, w&t.

Row 2 (WS): K19, w&t.

Row 3: K18, w&t.

Row 4: K17, w&t.

Continue working in this manner, knitting one fewer stitch before working the wrap and turn on each row, until there are 8 unwrapped stitches in the center of the heel.

Last Short-Row Decrease (RS): K7, w&t.

Short-Row Increases

Row 1 (WS): K8, w&t.

Row 2: K9, w&t.

Row 3: K10, w&t.

Row 4: K11, w&t.

Continue working in this manner, knitting one more stitch before working the wrap and turn on each row, until the first and last heels sts have been wrapped twice.

Last Short Row Increase (RS): K19, w&t. Now, there is one stitch on the right needle and 20 sts on the left needle.

Redistribute stitches as follows: Knit the next 10 heel

stitches onto the right needle (needle #4); the left needle, holding the remaining 10 heel stitches is now needle #1; remove the 19 instep sts from the waste yarn and divide them over two double-pointed needles (needles #2 and #3). You will now knit in the round again. The beginning of the round is at the center back of the sock.

54% of sock-o-holics said their favorite post-socks activity is starting another pair (of course!).

Pick-up round:

Needle #1: K10, pick up and k3 sts along the side of the heel flap—13 sts;

Needles #2 and #3: Work in established Rib & Garter Stitch pattern beginning with round 10 (when you work round 1 of the leg, needle #2 will begin with a purl stitch); pick up and k3 sts along the opposite side of the heel flap—19 sts;

Needle #4: Pick up and k3 sts along opposite side of heel flaps, knit to end—14 sts (46 sts total).

GUSSET

Round 1:

Needle #1: Knit to last 3 sts, k2tog, k1—12 sts;

Needles #2 and #3: Continue in Rib & Garter Stitch pattern as established;

Needle #4: K1, ssk, k to end—13 sts.

Round 2:

Needles #1 and #4: Knit to end;

Needles #2 and #3: Continue in Rib & Garter Stitch pattern as established.

Repeat last 2 rounds two more times—40 sts.

Repeat round 2 only until foot measures approx 2"/5cm less than the total desired length, measured from the back of the heel.

Shape Toe

Rounds 1, 3–7, 9–11, and 13: Knit.

Round 2: *K3, k2tog; repeat from * around—32 sts.

Round 8: *K2, k2tog; repeat from * around—24 sts.

Round 12: *K1, k2tog; repeat from * around—16 sts.

Round 14: *K2tog; repeat from * around—8 sts.

Note: For a neater finish to the toe, work round 14 with a 2.75mm (size 2 U.S.) needle.

Finish Toe

Cut yarn, leaving a 12"/30.5cm tail. Using the yarn needle, thread the yarn tail through the remaining stitches and pull it snug to close the opening.

FINISHING

Weave in ends.

Tip: The sock looks just as nice worn inside out.

This project was knit with:

Artyarns' Ultramerino 8, worsted weight, 100% hand-dyed merino wool, 3.5oz/100g = approx 188yd/169m per hank 2 hanks, UM8 117

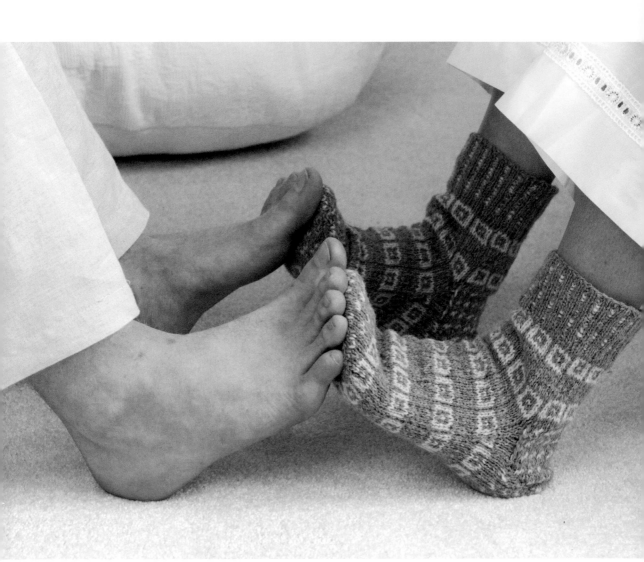

Toe to Toe

You'll be ready for some serious footsy action
wearing these captivating box-patterned socks.

by MAIA DISCOE

SKILL LEVEL
Intermediate

FINISHED MEASUREMENTS
Foot circumference 7¾ (8½, 9½)"/20 (22, 24)cm

Leg length 6¾ (7¼, 7¼)"/17 (18.5, 18.5)cm

Foot length 8½ (9, 9½)"/22 (23, 24)cm

MATERIALS AND TOOLS
Approx total: 588yd/537m of 🔵 fingering weight yarn, wool/nylon

Color A: 196yd/179m of 🔵 fingering weight yarn, wool, in green

Color B: 196yd/179m of 🔵 fingering weight yarn, wool, in yellow

Color C: 196yd/179m of 🔵 fingering weight yarn, wool, in orange

Knitting needles: 2.75mm (size 2 US) set of 5 double pointed needles, *or size to obtain gauge*

Stitch marker

Yarn needle

GAUGE
28 sts and 32 rows = 4"/10cm in Stockinette stitch (k every round)

Always take time to check your gauge.

Note: The ribbing and pattern stitch used in these socks are not very stretchy, due to stranding. For this reason, this pattern is not suited for tall socks.

CUFF
Cast on 54 (60, 66) sts. Distribute the stitches as follows: 12 (15, 15) sts each on needles #1 and #2 (for back of leg/sole), 15 (15, 18) sts each on needles #3 and #4 (for front of leg/instep). Place a stitch marker for beginning of round. Taking care not to twist stitches, join to work in the round.

Round 1: K1, *p1, k2; repeat from * to last st, k1.

Repeat round 1 for a total of 18 rounds, following Ribbing Chart.

LEG
Work Box Chart over 54 (60, 66) sts, for a total of 18 rounds (until the leg is a total of 3 boxes high and has 9 (10, 11) boxes around).

HEEL FLAP
Notes: Heel Flap is worked back and forth in rows over the 24 (30, 30) sts on needles #1 and #2. Work flap in St st (k on RS, p on WS) following Seed Chart. When working the last stitch of each row of the flap and heel turn, use both A and the contrasting color (B or C). Similarly, slip both strands as one stitch on following row.

Row 1 (RS): Begin Seed Chart, working over the 24 (30, 30) sts on needles #1 and #2 only, working last st using 1 strand each of A and the contrasting color (B or C), turn.

Row 2 (WS): Sl 1 (slip both strands), continue in Seed Chart over 24 (30, 30) sts on needles #1 and #2 only, working last st using 1 strand each of A and the contrasting color (B or C), turn.

Repeat last row for a total of 10 (12, 12) rows; end with a WS row.

ribbing chart

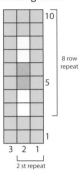

10

8 row repeat

5

1

3 2 1

2 st repeat

box chart

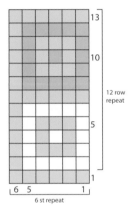

13

10

12 row repeat

5

1

6 5   1

6 st repeat

seed chart

4

4 row repeat

1

2 1

2 st repeat

(A) green
(B) yellow
(C) orange

Shape and Turn Heel

Note: Continue working the last stitch of each row using both A and the contrasting color, and slipping both strands as one stitch on the following row, throughout the heel turn.

Row 1: Sl 1, continue in Seed pattern as established until 3 sts remain on left needle, work next st with A and contrasting color, turn; leave last 2 sts unworked—22 (28, 28) active sts.

Repeat last row until there are 8 (10, 10) active sts; end with a WS row. There should be 8 (10, 10) unworked sts on each side of the active heel sts.

Next row (RS): Sl 1 as if to knit, continue in Seed pattern as established over 6 (8, 8) sts, k2tog, k1, turn.

Next row (WS): Sl 1 as if to purl, continue in Seed pattern as established over 7 (9, 9) sts, ssp, p1, turn.

Continue in this manner until all of the heel stitches have been incorporated; end with a WS row—16 (20, 20) sts.

GUSSET

Redistribute stitches as follows: With RS of heel facing, with a spare needle, continue in Seed pattern as established over the first 8 (10, 10) heel sts; with needle #2 continue in Seed pattern as established over the remaining 8 (10, 10) heel sts, with A pick up and k8 (9, 9) sts along side of heel flap; pick up and knit 1 st in the gap between the heel and the instep sts (gap stitch); with needles #3 and #4 continue in Box pattern as established across the instep sts; with needle #1 begin Box Chart beginning with stitch 2, pick up and knit 1 st in the gap between the instep and the heel sts (gap stitch); pick up and knit 8 (9, 9) sts along the opposite side of heel flap knit the 8 (10, 10) sts from the spare needle—64 (70, 76) sts.

Reposition:

Needle #2: Continue in Box pattern across to last st, with A knit last st.

Note: The last repeat of the Box pattern will be a partial repeat.

Needles #3 and #4: Work in established Box pattern across.

Notes: Take care to maintain Box pattern over instep and center heel stitches. Work partial repeats of the Box pattern in gusset stitches as needed.

Round 1:

Needle #1: Ssk, work in established pattern across.

Needle #2: Work in established pattern across to last 2 sts, k2tog;

Needles #3 and #4: Work in established pattern across—62 (68, 74) sts (16 (19, 19) sts each on needles #1 and #2, 15 (15, 18) sts each on needles #3 and #4).

Round 2: Knit all sts on all needles.

Round 3: Repeat Round 1—60 (66, 72) sts (15 (18, 18) sts

each on needles #1 and #2, 15 (15, 18) sts each on needles #3 and #4).

Repeat last 2 rounds until there are 12 (15, 15) sts remaining on each of needles #1 and #2—54 (60, 66) sts.

FOOT

Work even in Box pattern as established until foot measures 6½ (7, 7½)"/17 (18, 19)cm, measured from the center of the back heel; end with round 1 or round 7 of Box Chart.

Shape Toe

Round 1: [With A, ssk; work in Seed pattern over 23 (26, 29) sts; with A, k2tog] twice—50 (56, 62) sts.

Round 2: [With A, k1; work in Seed pattern over 23 (26, 29) sts; with A, k1] twice.

Round 3: [With A, ssk; work in Seed pattern over 21 (24, 27) sts; with A, k2tog] twice—46 (52, 58) sts.

Round 4: [With A, k1; work in Seed pattern over 21 (24, 27) sts; with A, k1] twice.

Continue in this manner until 18 (20, 22) sts remain.

48% of sock knitters prefer playing footsy with socks on.

Finish Toe

Place 9 (10, 11) stitches on each of two needles, with decreases at ends of needles. Use Kitchener Stitch to sew the two sets of stitches together.

FINISHING

Weave in ends. Wash in mild soap and block or lay flat to dry.

This project was knit with:

Harrisville's New England Shetland 2-ply Shetland wool, fingering weight, 100% wool, 1.75oz/50g = approx 196yd/179m per ball
(A) 1 ball, #7 tundra
(B) 1 ball, #6 cornsilk
(C) 1 ball, #4 gold

STITCH PATTERNS AND HAND-DYED YARN
BY SHANNON OKEY

If you're like most knitters, you've probably fallen in love with a hand-painted skein of sock yarn at some point, but what happens when you finally wind that ball of yarn and start knitting? Often the results are not what you expect—sometimes creating inconsistencies or pooling—but it's not always the yarn's fault. Stitch patterns have a strong effect on the final look of your project even when the yarn is only one color. The effect can be even more obvious when using multicolor yarns.

To illustrate this effect, here are four identical socks created with different stitch patterns: plain stockinette with a ribbed top, 2 x 2 ribbing, lace, and a small twisted cable pattern. The yarn is fingering weight Louet Gems superwash merino

that I dyed with acid dyes, pictured below. The socks are 68 stitches around (the cable sock has four additional stitches to accommodate its stitch pattern). The heels and top ribbed edge are all alike, and the bottom of each sock is stockinette.

When comparing the socks' overall color, each looks rosy pink and purple, but if you look closer you'll see a wide variety of differences. The stockinette sock appears lighter, having much more yellow than its siblings since there's no stitch pattern to "suck in" the yellow behind a rib or inside a cable. The ribbed sock has definitive color pooling in the green/gold shades—they stand out almost like incomplete color stripes. The cabled sock is perhaps the most balanced in terms of color: tight

little cables tend to wrap quite a bit of yarn out of immediate public view and redistribute the rest. On the lace sock, the openings inside the lace give your eye a visual rest so that you don't immediately spot the small, but attractive, pools of yellow and green across the top of the sock.

What can we learn from this? Don't despair if that precious skein of hand-dyed yarn isn't working out quite the way you think it should. Experimentation is good.

Shannon Okey is the author of more than 10 knitting and fiber-focused books, a columnist for knit.1 magazine, and frequent contributor to several other magazines. She can be found online at knitgrrl.com.

Socks knit by Andi Smith of Knit Brit.

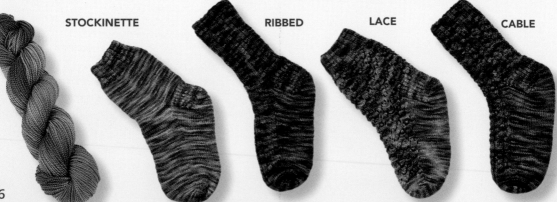

STOCKINETTE RIBBED LACE CABLE

Make-Up Socks

The only good thing about a lovers' quarrel? The make-up socks. With irresistible climbing vines up the front, back, and sides, these beauties will have him begging for mercy.

by KIRSTEN KAPUR

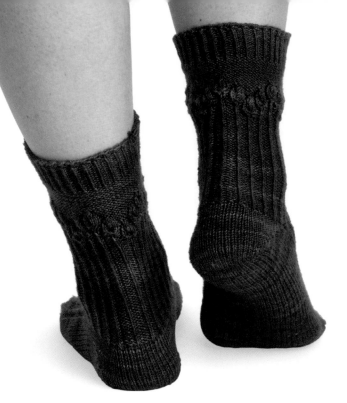

SKILL LEVEL
Experienced

FINISHED MEASUREMENTS
Foot circumference
7½"/19cm

Leg length 8"/20.5cm

Foot length custom

MATERIALS AND TOOLS
Approx total: 380yd/342m of
⬤ fingering weight yarn,
wool, in dark gold

Knitting needles: 2.25mm
(size 1 U.S.) 2 sets of
24"/61cm circular needles,
or size to obtain gauge

Stitch marker

Cable needle

Yarn needle

GAUGE
35 sts and 49 rows =
4"/10cm in Climbing Vine
Pattern (see chart)

*Always take time to check
your gauge.*

Note:
**Each sock is worked from
the toe up on two circular
needles.**

TOE
Using magic cast on, cast 9
sts onto each of two circular
needles—18 sts.

Round 1: Knit.

Round 2:

Needle #1: Kfb, knit to last
st, kfb.

Repeat for Needle #2.

Repeat this round until there
are 33 sts on each needle—66
sts.

FOOT
Next round:

Needle #1: Work row 1 of
Climbing Vine pattern from
chart.

Needle #2: Knit.

Next round:

Needle #1: Work next row of
Climbing Vine pattern from
chart.

Needle #2: Knit.

Continue working rounds
as established, repeating
chart rows 1–10, until sock is
2"/5cm less than desired foot
length.

twisted rib pattern (worked in the round, over multiples of 2 sts)

Round 1: *K1 tbl, p1; repeat from * around.
Repeat round 1 for Twisted Rib pattern.

Shape Heel
Notes:

1. To shape heel, short rows are worked back and forth on needle #2 only.

2. All slipped stitches are slipped purlwise.

Begin short row shaping:

Row 1 (RS): K32, w&t.

Row 2 (WS): P31, w&t.

Row 3: Knit to 1 st before wrapped st, w&t.

Row 4: Purl to 1 st before wrapped st, w&t.

Repeat rows 3 and 4 until there are 12 wrapped sts on each end, ending with a WS row.

Next row (RS): Knit to the nearest wrapped st, pick up wrap and knit together with the st, wrap next st (this stitch now has two wraps), turn.

Next row (WS): Purl to the nearest wrapped st, pick up wrap (from bottom to top on the RS of work) and purl together with st, wrap the next st (this stitch now has two wraps), turn.

Next row: Knit to the double-wrapped st, pick up the wraps and knit together with st, wrap the next st, turn.

Next row: Purl to the double-wrapped st, pick up the wraps and purl together with st, wrap the next st, turn.

Repeat last 2 rows until all wrapped stitches have been picked up.

LEG
Resume working in the round on both needles.

Next round:

Needle #1: Work next row of Climbing Vine pattern from chart (resuming from where you left off on the foot).

Needle #2: P1, *k1 tbl, p2; repeat from * 9 more times, k1 tbl, p1.

Continue working rounds as established, repeating chart rows 1–10, until four more repeats of the Climbing Vine chart have been completed.

Next round:

Needle #1: Begin working Top Border Front chart.

Needle #2: Begin working Top Border Back chart.

Continue working rounds as established, until all rows of Top Border charts have been completed.

CUFF
Work in Twisted Rib pattern for 14 rounds. Bind off loosely using a sewn bind off.

FINISHING
Weave in ends. Block if desired.

This project was knit with:

Shibui Knits' Sock, fingering weight, 100% superwash merino, 1.75oz/50g = approx 191yd/172m per skein 2 skeins, #S1395 Honey

off the charts

climbing vine

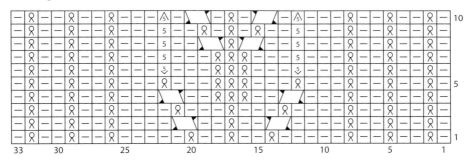

off the charts

climbing vine top border front

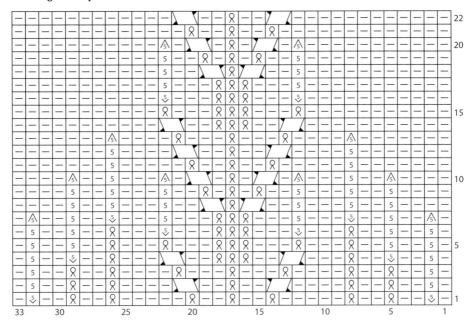

$\boxed{-}$	p on RS, k on WS
$\boxed{8}$	k tbl on RS, p tbl on WS
$\boxed{5}$	make 5 sts in one (k1, yo, k1, yo, k1) in one st
$\boxed{5}$	knit the 5 sts created in the increase st below
$\boxed{/s\backslash}$	s3k2p3: sl 3 as if to k3tog, k2tog, p3sso
	C2Bp tbl: Cable 2 back purl (k through back loop) - sl 1 st onto cn and hold in back, k1 tbl, p1 from cn
	C2Fp tbl: Cable 2 front purl (k through back loop) - sl 1 st onto cn and hold in front, p1, k1 tbl from cn

climbing vine top border back

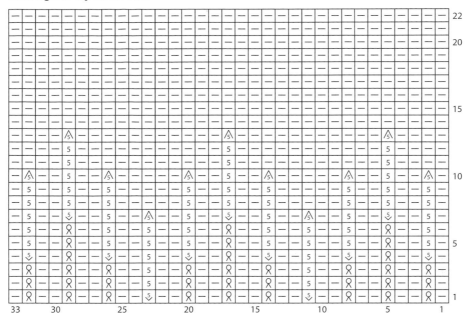

71

Royal Flush

On a winning streak? Expose your man's vulnerable side in a pair of ruby slippers…er, socks. The interlocking pattern down the front and back and the mildly demanding swirl pattern along the sides will make you the queen of hearts.

by MONA SCHMIDT

SKILL LEVEL
Intermediate

FINISHED MEASUREMENTS
Foot circumference
8½"/21.5cm

Leg length 7"/18cm

Foot length 8½"/21.5cm

MATERIALS AND TOOLS
Approx total: 324yd/292m of
1 sock weight yarn, wool,
in pink

Knitting needles: 2.5mm (size
1½ U.S.) set of 5 double-
pointed needles, or size to
obtain gauge

Stitch marker

Cable needle

Stitch holder

Yarn needle

GAUGE
30 sts and 44 rows = 4"/10cm
in Stockinette Stitch (knit
every round)

*Always take time to check
your gauge.*

Notes:
1. **Due to the twisted
   stitches, these socks do
   not stretch as much as
   socks knit in Stockinette
   Stitch. To get slightly
   larger socks, use 2.75mm
   (size 2 U.S.) needles with
   a gauge of 28 sts and
   44 rows = 4"/10cm in
   Stockinette Stitch. We
   recommend buying a third
   skein of yarn if making the
   larger socks.**
2. **All knit stitches of the
   charts are worked through
   the back loop, including
   knit stitches within cables
   and twists, unless otherwise stated.**

CUFF
Cast on 64 sts onto one
needle. Distribute the stitches
evenly over four needles
(16 sts per needle). Place a
stitch marker for beginning of
round. Taking care not to twist
stitches, join to work in the
round.

Rounds 1–8 (Ribbing): *K1,
p5, k2, p1, k1, p2, k2, p4, k2,
p2, k1, p1, k2, p5, k1; repeat
from * once more.

Leg
Note: When working chart B,
first work rows 1–16, then on
following repetitions work
rows 2–17.

Round 1 (charts): *Work first
row of chart A over next 8 sts,
p1, k1, work first row of chart
B over next 12 sts, k1, p1,
work first row of chart C over
next 8 sts; repeat from * once
more.

Rounds 2–16: *Work next row
of chart A over next 8 sts, p1,
k1, work next row of chart B
over next 12 sts, k1, p1, work
next row of chart C over next
8 sts; repeat from * once
more.

Round 17: *Work first row of
chart A over next 8 sts, p1, k1,
work second row of chart B
over next 12 sts, k1, p1, work
first row of chart C over next 8
sts; repeat from * once more.

Rounds 18–32: *Work next
row of chart A over next 8 sts,
p1, k1, work next row of chart
B over next 12 sts, k1, p1,
work next row of chart C over
next 8 sts; repeat from * once
more.

Slip stitches of needle #2 onto
needle #1, for a total of 32 sts
(for heel flap). Work heel flap
with needles #1 and #2 only.

Heel Flap

Row 1 (RS): Purl.

Row 2: Purl.

Row 3: *Sl 1, k1; repeat from * to end.

Row 4: Sl 1, purl remaining sts.

Rows 5–30: Repeat last 2 rows.

Turn Heel

Row 1 (RS): Sl 1, k17, k2tog tbl, k1, turn.

Row 2: Sl 1, p5, p2tog, p1, turn.

Row 3: Sl 1, k6, k2tog tbl, k1, turn.

Continue working in this manner, working one additional stitch before the decrease on each row, until 18 stitches remain, end with a WS row.

Note: On the last two rows, there will be no extra stitch to work after the decrease.

Pick-up round: With RS of heel facing and spare needle, knit first 9 heel sts; with another needle, knit the remaining 9 heel sts, pick up and k15 sts along side of heel flap (needle #1); with two more needles, continue in established cable pattern across 32 sts (needles #2 and #3—16 sts each); with another needle, pick up and k15 sts along opposite side of heel flap, k9 sts from spare needle (needle #4)—80 sts (24 sts each on needles #1 and #4, 16 sts each on needles #2 and #3).

Shape Gusset

Round 1:

Needle #1: Knit;

Needles #2 and #3: Continue in established cable pattern;

Needle #4: Knit.

Round 2:

Needle #1: Knit to last 2 sts, k2tog;

Needles #2 and #3: Continue in established cable pattern;

Needle #4: Ssk, knit to end—78 sts total.

Repeat last 2 rounds seven more times—64 sts.

Work rounds in established pattern, without further decreasing until 1 1/2 repeats of charts A, B, and C have been completed from instep pick-up row (through row 9 of each chart's row repeat).

Next 7 rounds:

Needle #1: Knit.

Needles #2 and #3: Work first 8 sts as they appear, p1, k1, work next row of chart B over next 12 sts, k1, p1, work last 8 sts as they appear.

Needle #4: Knit.

End ready to work stitches from needle #1.

Shape Toe

Round 1:

Needle #1: Knit to last 3 sts, k2tog, k1;

Needle #2: K1 tbl, k2tog tbl, continue in established pattern to end;

Needle #3: Continue in established pattern to last 3 sts, ssk tbl, k1 tbl;

Needle #4: K1, k2tog, knit to end—60 sts total.

Round 2:

Needle #1: Knit;

Needles #2 and #3: Continue in established cable pattern;

Needle #4: Knit.

Repeat rounds 1 and 2 seven more times—32 sts remain.

Repeat round 1 four times—16 sts remain.

Finish Toe

Knit stitches from needle #1 onto needle #4, and slip stitches from needle #3 onto needle #2. Cut yarn, leaving an 8"/20.5cm tail. Use Kitchener Stitch to sew the two sets of eight stitches together.

Finishing

Weave in ends.

Tip: When working with double-pointed needles, as you move from one needle to the next, cross the tip of the new needle over the tip of the needle just worked. Hold the yarn firmly when working the first stitch of the new needle. This will avoid "holes" in the finished piece.

This project was knit with:

Reynold's Soft Sea Wool, sock weight, 100% wool, 1.75oz/50g = approx 162yd/146m per skein 2 skeins, #941 hot pink

off the charts

chart a

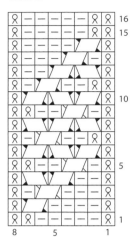

chart b

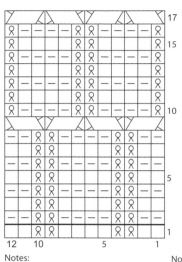

chart c

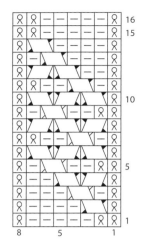

Note:
Work all k stitches through back loop.

Notes:
Work corresponding k sts
of cable through back loop.
Work rows 1-16 once, then work
rows 2-17 for following repeats.

Note:
Work all k stitches through back loop.

☐	k on RS, p on WS
⏀	k tbl on RS, p tbl on WS
−	p on RS, k on WS
◿◺	C3F: Cable 3 Front - sl 1 st onto cn and hold in front, k2, k1 from cn
◹◿	C3B: Cable 3 Back - sl 2 sts onto cn and hold in back, k1, k2 from cn
◺	LT: Left Twist - Cable 2 Front - sl 1 st onto cn and hold in front, k1, k1 from cn.
◺	C2Fp: Cable 2 Front purl - sl 1 st onto cn and hold in front, p1, k1 from cn
◹	C2Bp: Cable 2 Back purl - sl 1 st onto cn and hold in back, k1, p1 from cn

Hot Waves

Whether it's the jitterbug, the two-step, or the Charleston, these saucy socks are just too much fun to cover with your dancing shoes.

by LYNN HERSHBERGER

SKILL LEVEL
Intermediate

FINISHED MEASUREMENTS
Foot circumference 7 (7½, 8, 8½)"/18 (19, 20.5, 21.5)

Leg length 7"/18cm

Foot length 8½ (9¼, 10, 10¾)"/21.5 (23.5, 25.5, 27.5)cm

MATERIALS AND TOOLS
Approx total: 660yd/594m of ❶ fingering weight yarn, superwash wool/polyamide

> **Color A:** 220yd/198m of ❶ fingering weight yarn, super-wash wool/polyamide, in coral

> **Color B:** 220yd/198m of ❶ fingering weight yarn, super-wash wool/polyamide, in red

> **Color C:** 220yd/198m of ❶ fingering weight yarn, super-wash wool/polyamide, in purple

Knitting needles: 2mm (size 0 U.S.) set of 4 double-pointed needles, *or size to obtain gauge*

(optional) Knitting needles: 2.75mm (size 2 U.S.) set of 4 double-pointed needles (for the 9 rows of 2-color stranded knitting and/or for binding off).

(optional) Crochet hook: small crochet hook (for binding off)

Approx 1yd/1m smooth waste yarn, fingering weight cotton (or embroidery floss) in contrast color to B.

Yarn needle (with sharp point)

GAUGE
32 sts and 44 rows = 4"/10cm in Stockinette Stitch (knit every round)

Always take time to check your gauge.

Note: In this pattern, row gauge is essential to proper foot length.

With A, using the backward loop/e-wrap method, cast on 8 sts. Do not use a slip knot to start. Just hold the yarn with the needle in your right hand and start making loops. Note: This cast on is not bulky and is effective for a small number of sts. If you prefer, use a provisional cast on.

TOE RECTANGLE

This rectangle will become the very tip of your sock.

Row 1 (RS): Knit.

Rows 2, 4, 6, 8, and 10 (WS): Sl 1, purl across.

Rows 3, 5, 7, and 9: Sl 1, knit across.

Begin Knitting in the Round

With RS facing, k4 (half of total number of sts); with another needle k4 (remaining half of sts), pick up and knit 2 sts along the first half of the side edge (needle #1); with another needle pick up and knit 2 sts along the second half of the side edge, pick up and knit 8 sts along the cast-on edge, pick up and knit 2 sts along the first half of the second side edge (needle #2); with another needle, pick up and knit 2 sts along the second half of the second side edge, k4 from beginning of this process (needle #3). Beginning of round is between needles #3 and #1; place a marker here if desired.

Shape Toe

Continuing with A.

Round 1: Knit.

Round 2:

Needle #1: K to last st, m1, k1—7 sts.

Needle #2: K1, m1, k to last st, m1, k1—14 sts.

Needle #3: K1, m1, k to end—7 sts.

Repeat the last 2 rounds until there are 56 (60, 64, 68) sts.

FOOT

Begin working Toe Stripe pattern. When stripe pattern ends, work all rounds with B.

Continue in Stockinette st in the round (k every round) until sock measures 6½ (6¾, 7¼, 7¾)"/16.5 (17, 18.5, 20)cm from tip of toe.

toe stripe pattern

Knit 1 round with A, 5 rounds with B, 2 rounds with A, 3 rounds with B, 3 rounds with A, 2 rounds with B, 5 rounds with A, 1 round with B.

leg stripe pattern

Knit 1 round with C, 2 rounds with B, 3 rounds with C, 1 round with B, 1 round with C, 2 rounds with B, 3 rounds in Wave #1 pattern, 4 round with C, 1 round with B, 2 rounds with C, 2 rounds with B, 2 rounds with C, 3 rounds in Wave #2 pattern, 3 rounds with B, 2 rounds with C, 1 round with B, 1 round with C, 5 rounds with B, 2 rounds with A, 3 rounds with B, 1 round with A, 1 round with B, 2 rounds with A, 3 rounds with B, 3 rounds in Wave #3 pattern, 2 rounds with A, 1 round with B, 1 round with A.

wave #1 pattern

Round 1: *K3 with B, k3 with C; repeat from * around.

Round 2: K1 with C, *k2 with B, k1 with C, k1 with B, k2 with C; repeat from * to last 5 sts, k2 with B, k1 with C, k1 with B, k1 with C.

Round 3: K2 with C, *k3 with B, k3 with C; repeat from * to last 4 sts, k3 with B, k1 with C.

wave #2 pattern (reverse colors of Wave #1)

Round 1: *K3 with C, k3 with B; repeat from * around.

Round 2: K1 with B, *k2 with C, k1 with B, k1 with C, k2 with B; repeat from * to last 5 sts, k2 with C, k1 with B, k1 with C, k1 with B.

Round 3: K2 with B, *k3 with C, k3 with B; repeat from * to last 4 sts, k3 with C, k1 with B.

wave #3 pattern (Wave #1, with A substituted for C)

Round 1: *K3 with B, k3 with A; repeat from * around.

Round 2: K1 with A, *k2 with B, k1 with A, k1 with B, k2 with A; repeat from * to last 5 sts, k2 with B, k1 with A, k1 with B, k1 with A.

Round 3: K2 with A, *k3 with B, k3 with A; repeat from * to last 4 sts, k3 with B, k1 with A.

Next round: With C, knit.

Next round: With B, knit.

Next round: With B, k42 (45, 48, 51) (three-quarters of round), ending at side of sock.

Heel Preparation

Leave working yarn where it is, dangling at the side of the sock. Switch to waste yarn (slippery yarn in the same weight) and k28 (30, 32, 34) sts (half of circumference). Cut ends of waste yarn about 4"/10cm from sock and let hang to outside until later. Do not tie knots. Resume stitching where you left your working yarn, working stitches into the waste yarn just placed, and knit to end of round.

LEG

Continuing with B.

Round 1: Knit.

Round 2: Knit, dec 2 (0, 0, 0) and inc 0 (0, 2, 4) sts evenly spaced around—54 (60, 66, 72) sts.

Round 3: Knit.

Round 4: With C, knit.

Redistribute stitches placing 9 (10, 11, 12) sts on each needle. Work Leg Stripe pattern.

Note: When working wave patterns, consider using larger needles. Alternatively, work stitches with more relaxed tension than standard round, stretching the stitches on each needle after finishing all stitches. If you do not work the stranded-knitting wave pattern sts with a relaxed tension, the leg may not stretch over your heel.

ribbing stripe pattern

Rounds 1 and 2: With A, *k3, p1; repeat from * around.
Round 3: With B, knit.
Round 4: With B, *k3, p1; repeat from * around.
Round 5: With A, knit.
Rounds 6–11: Repeat round 1.
Round 12: With B, knit.
Round 13: With A, knit.
Rounds 14–17: Repeat round 1.

heel stripe pattern (toe stripe pattern with C substituted for A)

Knit 1 round with C, 5 rounds with B, 2 rounds with C, 3 rounds with B, 3 rounds with C, 2 rounds with B, 5 rounds with C, 1 round with B. Note: Depending on your size, the heel may end before/after the stripe sequence is complete. If you finish the sequence before heel is complete, work remaining rounds with C.

Rib

Transition round: Knit, dec 2 (0, 2, 0) sts evenly spaced around—52 (60, 64, 72) sts.

Redistribute stitches, placing 13 (15, 16, 18) sts on each needle. Work Ribbing Stripe pattern.

Stretchy Bind Off

During bind off, wrap stitches clockwise (rather than counterclockwise as is customary in western-style knitting).

Note to crocheters: This is how crochet wraps the yarn; you may prefer executing this bind off as a single crochet with a hook rather than using knitting instructions.

With a 2.75mm (size 2 U.S.) knitting needle or 2.75mm (size C-2 U.S.) crochet hook in your right hand, and wrapping your stitches clockwise, work 2 sts, *then insert left needle from left to right into the fronts of those 2 sts and k them together through the back loop, also wrapping that stitch clockwise, work next st and repeat from * until only 1 st remains on the right needle. Draw yarn tail through last st.

Note: The bind off will look flared until you block it or wear it, but you need that extra stretch in order for this sock to pull on over your heel.

Note: If you turn the sock upside down to pick up some stitches, you may end up with one extra stitch. You can decrease in the first knit round to adjust, if needed—56 (60, 64, 68) sts.

Once the stitches are secured, pick the waste yarn out of the gap between needles. You may cut the waste yarn ends in small bits as you remove it. When the waste yarn is completely removed, begin knitting in the round. If the stitches on the needles are seated incorrectly, adjust them as you work the first round.

Shape Heel

Begin working Heel Stripe pattern. If you complete the stripe sequence before completing the heel, work remaining rounds with C.

Rounds 1–3: Knit.

Decrease round:

Needle #1: K to last 3 sts, k2tog, k1—13 (14, 15, 16) sts;

Needle #2: K1, ssk, k to last 3 sts, k2tog, k1—26 (28, 30, 32) sts;

Needle #3: K1, ssk, k to end (beginning of round)—13 (14, 15, 16) sts.

Repeat last 4 rounds 2 (3, 4, 4) more times.

Next round: Knit.

Next round: Repeat decrease round.

Repeat last 2 rounds 1 (1, 1, 2) more times.

Repeat decrease round until 24 (24, 24, 28) sts remain.

off the charts

wave 1

wave 2

wave 3

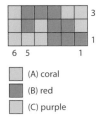

(A) coral
(B) red
(C) purple

Afterthought Heel

Note: This is not a standard afterthought heel and may look long and awkward when off the foot. The proof is in the wearing!

Holding your sock with the toe down and rib up, pick up your sock yarn stitches just above the waste yarn, 28 (30, 32, 34) sts on top of the waste yarn (needle #2). Pick up the right-side leg of the V-shaped stitches. Then pick up 14 (15, 16, 17) sts on each of 2 needles on the sts just below the waste yarn (still holding sock toe down) (needles #1 and #3).

Final Transition: K6 (6, 6, 7) sts until you reach the side of the sock. Cut yarn, leaving a 12"/30.5cm tail.

Slip stitches onto 2 needles only, placing 12 (12, 12, 14) instep stitches on one needle, and 12 (12, 12, 14) sole stitches on the other needle. Use Kitchener Stitch to sew the two sets of stitches together. Alternately, turn sock inside out and use a three-needle bind off (its minimal extra bulk is not typically detectable during wear).

FINISHING

Notice there are small gaps that form on either side at the top of the heel (where ends of waste yarn were located). With a sharp yarn needle and B, make a loop/drawstring on the inside around the hole. Once you stitch the loop around, pull the loop tight and pierce the drawstring with the needle on either side of the loop (cutting the circle in half). This will hold the hole closed.

Weave in ends. Block with water or steam, ideally drying on a sock blocker to maintain a recognizable foot shape while sock is flat.

This project was knit with:

Universal Yarn's Pace Step, fingering weight, 75% superwash wool/25% polyamide, approx 1.75oz/50g = 220yd/198m per ball
(A) 1 ball, #6401 coral
(B) 1 ball, #10 red
(C) 1 ball, #6403 purple

SOCKTALK LYNN HERSHBERGER on...socks on the go

"There is always a pair of socks in my bag. One time I went to the grocery store, parked, and walked half a block or so to the main entrance. The doors closed behind me, and I started to shop when I felt a tug as if I had caught a fish. I turned around and my sock yarn trailed behind me down the aisle, through the entryway, across the sidewalk, and past seven or eight cars to my car. I had dropped the ball of yarn in the car before shutting the door!"

From Russia with Love

by SaRi

Getting ready for a dinner and a show? On second thought, maybe it's better to just stay at home, pop in Doctor Zhivago, and heat things up with these mosaic-inspired socks.

SKILL LEVEL
Experienced

FINISHED MEASUREMENTS
Foot circumference 7 (7½, 8)"/18 (19, 20.5)cm

Leg length 8"/20.5cm

Foot length 10"/25.5cm

MATERIALS AND TOOLS
Approx total: 740yd/666m of 🔟 sock weight yarn, wool and wool/nylon/acrylic blend

Color A: 440yd/396m of 🔟 sock weight yarn, superwash wool/nylon/acrylic, in dark blue

Color B: 300yd/270m of 🔟 sock weight yarn, superwash wool, in variegated red-orange-yellow

Knitting needles: 2.5mm (size 1½ U.S.) set of 5 double-pointed needles; 3mm (size 2½ U.S.) set of 2 double-pointed needles, *or sizes to obtain gauge*

Stitch marker

Stitch holder

Yarn needle

GAUGE
36 sts and 34 rows = 4"/10cm in pattern worked in the round on 3mm (size 2½ U.S.) needles

28 sts and 40 rows = 4"/10cm in Stockinette Stitch (knit every round) on 2.5mm (size 1½ U.S.) needles

Always take time to check your gauge.

Notes:

1. These socks are worked in the round from the cuff down.

2. For the best result, the background color (A) should be carried above the pattern color strand (B). The pattern will show up better.

CUFF
With A and smaller needles, using the long tail cast-on method, cast on 64 (68, 72) sts. Distribute sts evenly over four needles (16 [17, 18] sts per needle). Place a stitch marker for beginning of round. Taking care not to twist sts, join to work in the round.

Knit 10 rounds.

Eyelet round: *K2tog, yo; repeat from * around.

Knit 2 rounds.

LEG
Change to larger needles. Continue knitting in rounds and, beginning on row 1, work 63 rows of chart 1.

Note: Work more or fewer rounds with chart, if a different leg length is desired.

HEEL FLAP
Redistribute stitches as follows: Continuing in established chart pattern, k32 (34, 36) sts onto one needle (for heel). The remaining stitches are held (for instep). Work back and forth over heel stitches only.

Row 1 (WS): Sl 1, p1 with A; continue in established chart pattern to last 2 sts of row; p2 with A.

Row 2 (RS): Sl 1, k1 with A; continue in established chart pattern to last 2 sts of row; k2 with A.

Repeat last 2 rows for a total of 27 (29, 31) rows; end with a WS row.

Turn Heel

Row 1 (RS): K21 (23, 25), skp, k1.

Row 2: P12 (14, 16), p2tog, p1.

Row 3: Knit to 1 st before gap, skp, k1, turn.

Row 4: Purl to 1 st before gap, p2tog, p1, turn.

Repeat rows 3 and 4 until all heel sts have been worked—22 (24, 26) sts.

GUSSET
Rejoin for working in the round as follows: With one needle, knit heel sts (needle #1); with another needle, pick up and k15 (16, 18) sts along side heel flap, alternating the two colors (needle #2); with another needle, continue in established chart 1 pattern over instep sts (needle #3); with another needle, pick up and k15 (16, 18 sts) along op-

off the charts
chart 1 (over 64 stitches)

posite side of heel flap, alternating the two colors (needle #4)—84 (90, 98) sts (22 [24, 26] sts on needle #1, 15 [16, 18] sts on needle #2, 32 [34, 36] sts on needle #3, 15 [16, 18] sts on needle #4).

Round 1:

Needles #1, #2, and #4:

Work row 1 of checkerboard chart over all sts.

Needle #3: Continue in established chart 1 pattern.

Round 2 (decrease round):

Needle #1: Continue in checkerboard pattern over all sts.

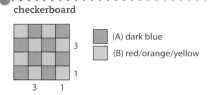
(A) dark blue
(B) red/orange/yellow

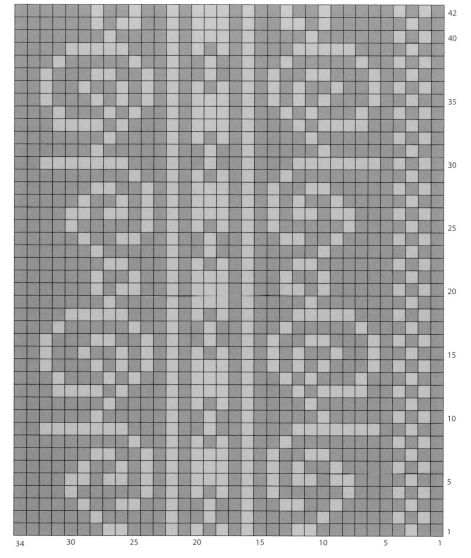

Toe Decrease:

Needles #1 and #3: Knit to last 3 sts, k2tog, k1.

Needles #2 and #4: K1, skp, k to end.

Continue in established patterns, repeating toe decrease on 5th, 8th, 11th, 13th, 15th, and 17th round. Then repeat toe decrease every round until 8 sts remain (2 sts per needle). Cut yarn and weave through remaining 8 sts, and pull tight to secure.

FINISHING

Weave in ends. Fold cuff at eyelet round to form picot top edge, and sew hem at top of cuff to WS. Block if desired.

Tip: When working with double-pointed needles, as you move from one needle to the next, cross the tip of the new needle over the tip of the needle just worked. Hold the yarn firmly when working the first stitch on the new needle. This will avoid "holes" in the finished piece.

This project was knit with:

Lang Jawoll's Sock Yarn including reinforcement yarn, sock weight, 75% superwash new wool/18% nylon/7% acrylic, approx 1.5oz/45g = 220yd/198m per ball (A) 2 balls, #47869 dark blue Wollmeise's Hand-Dyed Sockyarn "superwash," sock weight, 100% superwash wool, approx 5.25oz/150g = 575yd/518m per skein. (B) 1 skein, Bob

Needle #2: Continue in checkerboard pattern to last 2 sts, skp—14 (15, 17) sts.

Needle #3: Continue in established chart 1 pattern.

Needle #4: K2tog, continue in checkerboard pattern to end—14 (15, 17, 25) (82 [88, 96] sts total).

Repeat the last 2 rounds until 64 (68, 72) sts remain.

FOOT

Redistribute sts evenly over 4 needles (16 [17, 18] sts per needle) as follows: Maintaining patterns as established, knit first half of heel sts onto a holder; knit second half of heel sts and gusset sts of needle #2 onto one needle (needle #1); knit instep sts of needle #3 evenly distributed over 2 needles (needles #2 and #3); knit gusset sts of needle #4 and first half of heel sts (on holder) onto another needle (needle #4). Place marker at middle of the heel (between needles #1 and #4); this is the beginning of the round.

Continue to work in patterns as established until foot measures 2"/5cm less than desired length.

Shape Toe

Ensure that stitches are divided evenly, with checkerboard stitches on needles #1 and #4, and chart 1 stitches on needles #2 and #3. Maintain established patterns throughout.

off the charts

chart 1 (over 72 stitches)

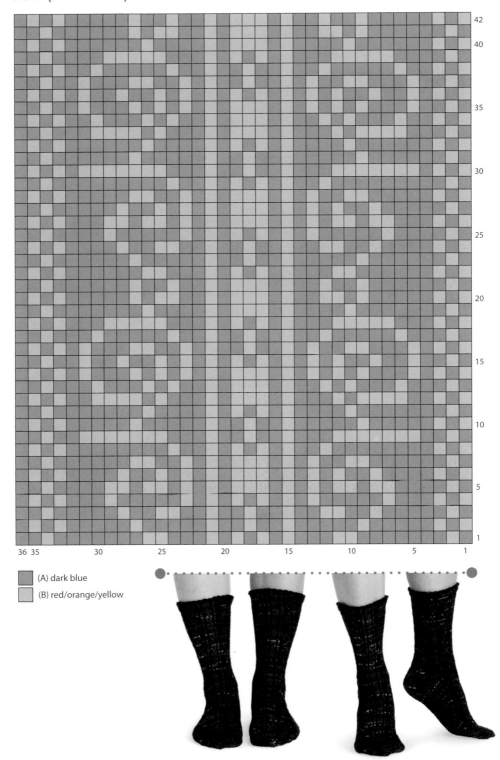

- (A) dark blue
- (B) red/orange/yellow

MY FIRST TIME

BY LAURIE PERRY, CRAZYAUNTPURL.COM

Although I'd never given much thought to it until I started knitting, my history with socks is pretty average, as is my collection. I have the usual suspects: low-cut plain white tennis socks, a couple of cutesy pairs, a trouser sock or two, mounds of basic athletic socks, and, if I'm not mistaken, one lonely pair of argyle knee socks sits in the corner of my sock drawer, waiting anxiously for the '80s to make a roaring comeback.

To my previously untrained eye, the lowly sock was nothing more than a stretchy fabric cover-up for my bad pedicure days. Even when I first started knitting, I passed right over the sock yarns because, honestly, I don't really need cozy hand-knit socks here in the arctic wilds of Southern California. I guess I hadn't considered that folks actually knit a whole sock, not to mention two whole socks, until I took up knitting and met them—The Sock People.

Once you begin knitting and move past the prerequisite "Major Scarf Phase," you start to encounter The Sock People. It seems like there is a whole posse of passionate DPN-wielding knitters out there, waving their yarn lassos and trying to rope us all in. They're in yarn shops, at knitting groups, and in your "How To Knit With Cables" class, all talking about mystical things like toe-ups and heel flaps and trying to lure us in with tall tales about socks being portable, easy, and oh-so-satisfying. And they are all a little more evolved than my brand of knitting, which is "Buy yarn because it's pretty and realize you only have enough to make a scarf—a very skinny scarf."

But I finally fell into the snare of these sock-knitting enthusiasts. I bought a pattern, some yarn, and some emergency wine, just in case. After all, if I messed up somewhere in the middle and made a heel of myself—sock knitting is so punny!—no one was going to show up on my doorstep and take me into custody for crimes against knitting. Probably. Right?

I started with a swatch, which is an especially good place to start when one is an insanely tight knitter like myself. From the cramped little stitches on my needles you can safely assume I took up knitting as a mode of therapy. When I finally found the correct needle size for the pattern's required gauge—two needle sizes bigger than the pattern called for—I cast on and started my first cuff.

Casting on was relatively painless, a simple knit-one-purl-one ribbing, but working with double-pointed needles felt kind of extreme. The honeymoon phase—the cuff and body of the sock—lasted about two bus rides, an odorous, arduous commute that's also good knitting time. When I got to the part of the pattern where I needed to turn the heel, I was bumping along in rocky traffic with my pattern slipping off my lap, my stitch counter rolling around on the seat, and some strong language forming in my mind. After about 15 minutes of slipped stitches and almost poking my seatmate in the eye, it dawned on me that I was doing this intentionally—making a heel flap on a moving, lurching, metro bus.

Later—after the emergency wine supply had been breached—I realized that this experience taught me an important lesson: when you turn a heel, sit somewhere quiet and placid that's full of stable, non-moving surfaces. With my first heel turned, I began to realize that this whole sock-knitting endeavor is a bit like making magic. I felt as if I had single-handedly built Stonehenge or something—picking up stitches, knitting halfway through a row and knitting back again, shaping the heel with short rows, yet using your basic ol' knit and purl with a few increases and decreases.

It was very exciting and I tried to share my excitement with my co-workers. "Hey, I know we're in a meeting to discuss a spreadsheet, but you guys! Guess what! I made a sock!"

I made it through the heel flap, through a cat chewing one of my double-pointed needles, through the cross-town bus fiasco, and through my first gusset. By the time I reached the toe, I was so full of myself that my knitting ego had to ride shotgun in the car.

"I MADE A WHOLE SOCK!" I informed my dad. "A whole entire sock! By hand! With just yarn and knitting needles!"

"That's great," said my dad. "But don't you have two feet?"

There is, however, one thing The Sock People forget to mention. Sure, you'll love knitting up a sock—the portability, the quickness, the addiction—and you may even be a little amazed at yourself and your skills. But what they don't tell you is that the second sock is a lonely, desolate outpost of obligation. That second sock is just the stepchild of the first sock's exuberance.

Oh, the second sock!

Laurie Perry is a Southerner of mixed pedigree, from Texas, Louisiana, Mississippi, and every small town in between. Her work has been featured in two collections of essays, and her first full-length book, *Drunk, Divorced & Covered in Cat Hair*, was released in 2007. She knits and writes in Los Angeles, where she chronicles her life in an online diary, CrazyAuntPurl.com.

Big Tease

SKILL LEVEL
Intermediate

FINISHED MEASUREMENTS
Foot circumference 8"/20.5cm

Leg length 8"/20.5cm

Foot length 8½"/21.5cm

MATERIALS AND TOOLS
Approx total: 382yd/344m of
 fingering weight yarn,
superwash merino, in ivory

Knitting needles: 2.5mm
(size 1½ U.S.) set of 5
double-pointed needles, and
1 needle 2–3 sizes larger (for
binding off),
or size to obtain gauge

Crochet hook: 2–3mm (sizes
B/1–D/3 U.S.).

Waste yarn (for provisional
cast on)

Yarn needle

GAUGE
32 sts and 44 rows = 4"/10cm
in Stockinette Stitch (knit
every round)

*Always take time to check your
gauge.*

Special Abbreviations
Slip 2, knit 1, pass 2 slipped sts
over (s2kp2): Slip 2 stitches
as if to knit 2 stitches
together, knit 1, pass both
slipped stitches over (2
stitches decreased).

by AMY POLCYN

Mmmm... white arrow lace socks—
fresh, pure, and pristine. Keep them
that way by enlisting a personal
transportation assistant.

TOE

With waste yarn and crochet hook, chain 36. Fasten off.

With project yarn and two double-pointed needles, pick up 32 sts through chain (1 st per chain, leaving a couple empty chains on each end).

Row 1 (WS): Purl to last st, w&t.

Row 2: Knit to last st, w&t.

Row 3: Purl to 1 st before wrapped st, w&t.

Row 4: Knit to 1 st before wrapped st, w&t.

Repeat last 2 rows until there are 8 wrapped sts on each end, ending with a RS row.

Next row (WS): Purl to nearest wrapped st, pick up wrap and work together with st, turn.

Next row: Sl 1, knit to nearest wrapped st, pick up wrap and work together with st, turn.

Repeat last 2 rows until all wraps have been picked up.

FOOT

Cut waste yarn and remove. Place live stitches (32 stitches on needle and 32 stitches revealed from removing waste yarn) evenly distributed on four double-pointed needles (16 stitches per needle). Join to work in the round.

Round 1: Knit, inc 1 st at end of needle #2—65 sts (33 instep sts, 32 heel sts).

Work Arrow Lace pattern on needles #1 and #2 (instep) and Stockinette st on needles #3 and #4 (heel), ending instep sts by repeating first st of round to balance pattern. Continue as established until foot measures 7"/18cm (or approx 2"/5cm less than desired length), ending with round 16 of pattern.

HEEL

Working back and forth on needles #3 and #4 only (leave sts on needles #1 and #2 on hold), repeat instructions for toe, beginning with row 1.

twisted ribbing (worked in the round, over multiples of 2 sts)

Round 1: *P1, k1 tbl; repeat from * around.
Repeat round 1 for Twisted Ribbing pattern.

arrow lace (multiples of 8 sts)

Round 1 and all odd-numbered rounds: Knit.
Round 2: *K1, yo, ssk, k3, k2tog, yo; repeat from * around.
Round 4: *K2, yo, ssk, k1, k2tog, yo, k1; repeat from * around.
Round 6: *P1, k2, yo, s2kp2, yo, k2; repeat from * around.
Rounds 8, 10, 12, 14, and 16: *P1, ssk, k1, yo, k1, yo, k1, k2tog; repeat from * around.
Repeat rounds 1–16 for Arrow Lace pattern.

64% of sock knitters readily admit to having a yarn addiction problem. The 3% who said they don't were probably lying.

SOCK TALK AMY POLCYN on...socks on the go

" I keep an emergency sock in my purse at all times so I'm never without my knitting. Socks are perfect on-the-go projects. I knit socks at the playground, long lines at the bank or grocery store, at the movies...anywhere! "

off the charts

arrow lace

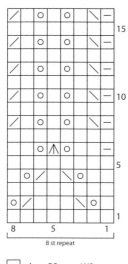

8 st repeat

☐ k on RS, p on WS
☐ p on RS, k on WS
☐ yarn over
☐ k2tog
☐ ssk

LEG

Resume working in the round.

Round 1: Knit, working last 2 sts of needle #2 together—64 sts (32 instep sts, 32 heel sts).

Work Arrow Lace pattern, beginning with round 2, on all sts until leg measures 7"/18cm or desired length from heel, ending with round 16 of pattern.

Next round: Knit.

Cuff

Work Twisted Rib pattern for 1"/2.5cm. Bind off loosely using larger needle.

FINISHING

Weave in ends. Block if desired.

This project was knit with:

Shibui Knits' Sock, fingering weight, 100% superwash merino, 1.75oz/50g = approx 191yd/172m per skein 2 skeins, #S7501 Ivory

Puppy
Love

When you're getting your dog ready for a bit of park trolling, climb into these lacey holed socks with reptile trim— perfect for rubber clogs.

by PAULINE SCHULTZ

SKILL LEVEL
Intermediate

FINISHED MEASUREMENTS
Foot circumference 6¼ (7¼, 8½)"/16 (18.5, 21.5)cm

Leg length 4½ (6, 7¾")/11.5 (15, 19.5)cm

Foot length 8½ (9½, 10)"/21.5 (24, 25.5)cm

MATERIALS AND TOOLS
Approx total: 420yd (378) m of ❶ fingering weight yarn, wool, in lime

Knitting needles: 2.75mm (size 2 U.S.) set of 4 double-pointed needles, *or size to obtain gauge*

Stitch marker

Yarn needle

GAUGE
30 sts and 42 rows = 4"/10cm in Stockinette Stitch (knit every round)

30 sts and 48 rows = 4"/10cm in Lace Stitch pattern

Always take time to check your gauge.

CUFF
Using provisional cast on of your choice, cast on 44 (52, 60) sts. Distribute stitches evenly over three double-pointed needles. Taking care not to twist stitches, mark beginning and join to work in the round.

Knit 2 rounds.

Make Teeth
Note: Teeth are worked back and forth in rows.
Row 1 (RS): P2, turn.

Row 2: P2 (or k2 backwards).

Row 3: P3.

Row 4: P3 (or k3 backwards).

Row 5: P4.

Row 6: P4 (or k4 backwards).

Row 7: Bind off 4 sts, p1.

Repeat rows 2–7 around, ending last repeat; bind off 3 sts. Pick up and purl the purl bump of the first stitch of the round. Pass the third bound-off stitch over this stitch, cut the yarn and draw through—11 (13, 15) "teeth."

With RS facing, pick up 44 (52, 60) sts from the provisional cast on. Join yarn and work in K1, p1 Rib for ¾ (1, 1½")/2 (2.5, 4)cm. Remove provisional cast-on yarn after a few rounds.

ANKLE
Work rounds 1–6 of Lace Pattern (in rounds) 4 (6, 8) times, then work rounds 1–3 once more.

HEEL FLAP
Note: The heel flap is worked back and forth in rows over 13 (17, 21) sts. The remaining sts are held for later (instep sts).

Next row: M1, k1 tbl, *k3, k1 tbl; repeat from * 2 (3, 4) more times, m1—15 (19, 23) sts.

Work rows 2–6 of Lace Pattern (in rows), then work all 6 rows of the pattern 2 (3, 4) more times.

Turn Heel
Row 1: K11 (13, 15) sts, turn.

Row 2: Sl 1, p3, p2tog, p1, turn.

Row 3: Sl 1, k4, ssk, k1, turn.

Row 4: Sl 1, p5, p2tog, p1, turn.

Continue working in this manner working one additional stitch before the decrease on each row, until 10 (12, 14) sts remain; end with a WS row.

GUSSET
Slip all instep stitches onto a free needle; with another needle, knit across half the heel sts. Resume working in the round.

Pick-up round:

Needle #1: Knit across remaining 5 (6, 7) heel sts, pick up and knit 10 (12, 14) sts up the side of the heel flap—15 (18, 21) sts.

Needle #2: M1, work round 4 of Lace pattern (in rounds), m1—33 (37, 41) sts.

Needle #3: Pick up and knit 10 (12, 14) sts down other side of the heel flap, knit to end—15 (18, 21) sts.

You are now at center back of sock.

Next round:

Needle #1: Knit to last 3 sts, k2tog, k1—14 (17, 20) sts.

Needle #2: Continue with Lace pattern (in rounds), end k1 tbl.

Needle #3: K1, ssk, knit to end of round—14 (17, 20) sts.

Next round:

Needle #1: Knit.

Needle #2: Continue with Lace pattern (in rounds), end k1 tbl.

Needle #3: Knit.

Repeat last 2 rounds until 47 (55, 63) sts remain. Continue without further decreasing until sock measures 7½ (8½, 9)"/19 (21.5, 23)cm from heel, ending with row 1 or row 3 of Lace pattern.

TOE

Redistribute stitches on needles, as follows:

Needle #1: K11 (13, 15).

Needle #2: K1, ssk, k9 (11, 13), ssk, k8 (10, 12), k2tog, k1—22 (26, 30) sts.

Needle #3: K11 (13, 15).

Decrease round:

Needle #1: Knit to last 3 sts, k2tog, k1—10 (12, 14) sts.

Needle #2: K1, ssk, k to last 3 sts, k2tog, k1—20 (24, 28) sts.

Needle #3: K1, ssk, k to end—10 (12, 14) sts.

Next round: Knit all sts on all needles.

Repeat decrease round until 32 (36, 44) sts remain. Repeat last 2 rounds until 16 (20, 24) sts remain.

Finish Toe

Knit all sts on needle #1. Slip sts of needle #1 and needle #2 onto one needle. You should have 8 (10, 12) sts each on two needles. Hold sts on two needles parallel. Use 3-needle bind off or Kitchener Stitch to join the two sets of stitches.

FINISHING

Weave in ends. Block if desired.

Tip: To avoid continually turning the sock as you knit the "teeth," learn how to knit backwards, as follows:

Take yarn to back; insert left needle into stitch behind right needle; bring yarn around in front of left needle from left to right and draw yarn through; drop stitch from right needle. Repeat across row.

This project was knit with:

Cherry Tree Hill's Supersock solids, fingering weight, 100% merino wool, 4oz/112g = approx 420yd/378m per ball
1 ball, Lime

lace pattern (worked in the round, over multiples of 4 sts)

Round 1: *K1 tbl, p3; repeat from * around.
Round 2: *K1 tbl, p2tog, yo, k1; repeat from * around.
Round 3: Repeat round 1.
Rounds 4–6: *K1 tbl, k3; repeat from * around.

lace pattern (worked in rows, over multiples of 4 sts + 3)

Row 1: K1, *k1 tbl, k3; repeat from * to last 2 sts, k1 tbl, k1.
Row 2: P1, *p1 tbl, p3; repeat from * to last 2 sts, p1 tbl, p1.
Row 3: Repeat row 1.
Row 4: P1, *p1 tbl, k3; repeat from * to last 2 sts, p1 tbl, p1.
Row 5: K1, *k1 tbl, p2tog, yo, k1; repeat from * to last 2 sts, k1 tbl, k1.
Row 6: Repeat row 4.

Girl's Best Friend Thigh Highs

With a single pair of socks—accented with a lace detail on both sides that goes all the way up—you can cross three super-hot must-haves off your list: thigh highs, lace, and diamonds.

SKILL LEVEL
Experienced

FINISHED MEASUREMENTS
Foot circumference 7½ (8,
  8½)"/19 (20.5, 21.5)cm

Calf circumference 10 (12,
  14)"/25.5 (30.5, 36)cm

Leg length custom

Foot length custom

MATERIALS AND TOOLS
Approx total: 1100yd/990m
  of (1) fingering weight
  yarn, wool/mohair/nylon
  blend, purple heather variegated

Knitting needles: 2.25mm
  (size 1 U.S.) set of 5
  double-pointed needles,
  and 2mm (size 0 U.S.) set of
  5 double pointed needles,
  or size to obtain gauge

Stitch markers

Yarn needle

GAUGE
36 sts and 50 rows = 4"/10cm
  in Stockinette Stitch (knit
  every round) using 2.25mm
  (size 1 U.S.) needles

*Always take time to check
  your gauge.*

by STAR ATHENA

Turn Toe

Row 1: K14 (16, 18); pick up the wrap around the next stitch and knit it together through the back loop with the stitch it is wrapped around, w&t.

Row 2: P15 (17, 19); pick up the wrap around the next stitch and purl it together with the stitch it is wrapped around, w&t.

Row 3: K16 (18, 20); pick up both wraps around the next stitch and knit them together through the back loop with the stitch it is wrapped around, w&t.

Row 4: P17 (19, 21); pick up both wraps around the next stitch and purl them together with the stitch it is wrapped around, w&t.

Continue as established until you have worked all 34 (36, 38) stitches.

Pick up the 34 (36, 38) stitches remaining from your provisional cast on—68 (72, 76) sts. Distribute sts evenly over four needles (17 [18, 19] sts per needle). Place a stitch marker for beginning of round. Join to work in the round.

Note: Two of the needles hold stitches for the top of the foot; the other two needles hold the stitches for the bottom of the foot.

FOOT

Knit every round until foot measures 2"/5cm less than desired foot length. Note: Slip the round marker each time you come to it, or place a coil-less safety pin on your sock to indicate where the end of the round is, to avoid having to slip a marker every round.

HEEL

Note: The heel is worked back and forth over 34 (36, 38) sts. Hold the instep stitches on the needles, or slip them to a stitch holder or waste yarn if you prefer to keep these needles out of your way.

Row 1 (RS): K33 (35, 37), w&t.

Row 2 (WS): P32 (34, 36), w&t.

Continue as established for a total of 20 rows, ending with a WS row. There should be 14 (16, 18) unwrapped sts at the center of the needles.

Turn Heel

Row 1 (RS): K14 (16, 18); pick up the wrap around the next stitch and knit it together through the back loop with the stitch it is wrapped around, w&t.

Row 2: P15 (17, 19); pick up the wrap around the next stitch and purl it together with the stitch it is wrapped around, w&t.

Row 3: K16 (18, 20); pick up both wraps around the next stitch and knit them together through the back loop with the stitch it is wrapped around, w&t.

TOE

With 2.25mm (size 1 U.S.) needles, cast on 34 (36, 38) sts using a provisional cast on. Purl back across these stitches.

Row 1 (RS): K33 (35, 37), w&t.

Row 2 (WS): P32 (34, 36), w&t.

Row 3: K31 (33, 35), w&t.

Row 4: P30 (32, 34), w&t.

Continue as established for a total of 20 rows, ending with a WS row. There should be 14 (16, 18) unwrapped sts at the center of the needle.

Row 4: P17 (19, 21); pick up both wraps around the next stitch and purl them together with the stitch it is wrapped around, w&t.

Continue as established until you have worked all 34 (36, 38) stitches.

LEG

You are now ready to start knitting in the round again. If you have put the top of the foot stitches onto a stitch holder or waste yarn, put them back onto the needles. Knit across top of foot (needles #3 and #4) back to the beginning of the next round (the beginning of the heel stitches). Knit one round.

Round 1 (redistribute stitches): With spare needle, k8 (9, 10); with another needle k9 sts, place marker, k8 (9, 10) (needle #1); with another needle k17 (18, 19) (needle #2); with another needle k17 (18, 19) (needle #3); with another needle k9 sts, then k8 (9, 10) from spare needle (needle #4). Complete round as follows:

Needle #1: Knit;

Needle #2: Work row 1 of Diamond Lace pattern;

Needle #3: Knit;

Needle #4: Work row 1 of Diamond Lace pattern.

Round 2:

Needle #1: Knit;

Needle #2: Work next row of Diamond Lace pattern;

Needle #3: Knit;

Needle #4: Work next row of Diamond Lace pattern.

Repeat round 2 until leg measures desired length to calf shaping (approx 6"/15cm is good for most people). Note: You will want to think about the shape of your leg and make adjustments as needed, beginning the increases earlier or later if you have shorter or longer legs, or narrower or wider calves. Try the sock on often to ensure a good fit. The directions included are for a semi-snug fit on the calf, so the socks stay in place.

Shape Calf

Increase round: Knit to marker at center of needle #1 (back of leg), insert right needle into stitch just below the stitch you just knitted into and knit into that stitch also, m1 (2 sts increased), complete round in pattern as established—70 (74, 78) sts. Note: The 2 increased sts should be in the center of needle #1.

Continue as established, repeating increase round every 6 rounds 9 (15, 21) times—88 (104, 120) sts.

Note: You may find managing all of the increases on needle #1 to be difficult after a while. You can slide some of these stitches onto needle #2 and needle #4 for ease, but you'll probably want to place a marker first, so you can be sure to continue following the Diamond Lace pattern without getting confused by the extra stitches.

Continue even as established until leg reaches just above the widest part of your calf.

diamond lace pattern (over 17 [18, 19] stitches)

. . . .

Row 1: K7 (8, 8), k2tog, yo, k8 (8, 9).

Row 2 and all even rows: Knit.

Row 3: K6 (7, 7), k2tog, yo, k1, yo, ssk, k6 (6, 7).

Row 5: K5 (6, 6), k2tog, yo, k3, yo, ssk, k5 (5, 6).

Row 7: K4 (5, 5), k2tog, yo, k5, yo, ssk, k4 (4, 5).

Row 9: K3 (4, 4), k2tog, yo, k7, yo, ssk, k3 (3, 4).

Row 11: K3 (4, 4), yo, ssk, k7, k2tog, yo, k3 (3, 4).

Row 13: K4 (5, 5), yo, ssk, k5, k2tog, yo, k4 (4, 5).

Row 15: K5 (6, 6), yo, ssk k3, k2tog, yo, k5 (5, 6).

Row 17: K6 (7, 7), yo, ssk, k1, k2tog, yo, k6 (6, 7).

Row 19: K7 (8, 8), yo, ssk, k8 (8, 9).

Row 20: Knit.

Ribbing

Change to 2mm (size 0 U.S.) needles.

Next round: *P2, k2; repeat from * around.

Repeat last round until leg reaches just above the knee.

Shape Thigh

Note: You will want to think about the shape of your thigh and make adjustments as needed, beginning the increases earlier or later or working more or fewer increases for the best fit. Try the sock on often to ensure a good fit. The directions included are for a semi-snug fit on the thigh, so the socks stay in place.

Round 1 (increase round): Work to center back; insert right needle into stitch just below the stitch you just knit into and knit into that stitch also, place marker, k1, m1. Redistribute the stitches so that this point is the end of the round—90 (106, 122) sts.

Round 2: *P2, k2; repeat from * to last 2 sts, k2.

Round 3 (increase round): *P2, k2; repeat from * around to marker; insert right needle into stitch just below the stitch you just knit into and purl into that stitch, slip marker, m1, k2—92 (108, 124) sts.

Rounds 4–8: *P2, k2; repeat from * around.

Round 9 (increase round): *P2, k2; repeat from * around to 1 st before marker, p1; insert right needle into stitch just below the stitch you just purled into and purl into that stitch also, slip marker, p1; insert

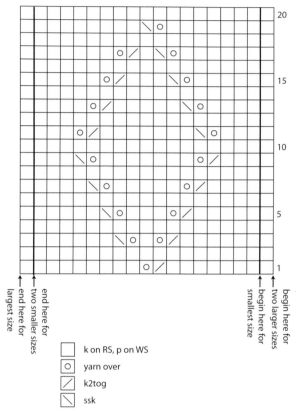

diamond lace

k on RS, p on WS
○ yarn over
╱ k2tog
╲ ssk

begin here for two larger sizes
begin here for smallest size
end here for two smaller sizes
end here for largest size

right needle into stitch just below the stitch you just purled into and purl into that stitch also, k2—94 (110, 126) sts.

Round 10: *P2, k2; repeat from * to last 6 sts, p4, k2.

Round 11 (increase round): *P2, k2; repeat from * around to 2 sts before marker, p2; insert right needle into stitch just below the stitch you just purled into and knit into that stitch, slip marker, m1, p2, k2—96 (112, 128) sts.

Rounds 12–16: *P2, k2; repeat from * around.

Round 17 (increase round): *P2, k2; repeat from * around

to 3 sts before marker, p2, k1; insert right needle into stitch just below the stitch you just knit into and knit into that stitch also, slip marker, k1, m1, k2, p2, k2—98 (114, 130) sts.

Round 18: *P2, k2; repeat from * to last 6 sts, k2, p2, k2.

Round 19 (increase round): *P2, k2; repeat from * around to marker; insert right needle into stitch just below the stitch you just knit into and purl into that stitch, slip marker, m1, k2, p2, k2—100 (116, 132) sts.

Rounds 20–24: *P2, k2; repeat from * around.

Round 25 (increase round): *P2, k2; repeat from * around to 1 st before marker, p1; insert right needle into stitch just below the stitch you just purled into and purl into that stitch also, slip marker, p1; insert right needle into stitch just below the stitch you just purled into and purl into that stitch also, k2, p2, k2—102 (118, 134) sts.

Round 26: *P2, k2; repeat from * to last 10 sts, p4, k2, p2, k2.

Round 27 (increase round): *P2, k2; repeat from * around to 2 sts before marker, p2; insert right needle into stitch just below the stitch you just purled into and knit into that stitch, slip marker, m1, [p2, k2] twice—104 (120, 136) sts.

Rounds 28–32: *P2, k2; repeat from * around.

Note: Try the sock on and determine whether you need to work more increases. Remember, you want the sock snug but not uncomfortable. If you need a wider thigh, work more increases as established. Otherwise continue in P2, k2 Rib until about 5"/12.5cm above the knee.

FINISHING

Bind off using a stretchy sewn bind off. Weave in ends. Block if desired.

This project was knit with:

Schaefer Anne Yarn's, fingering weight, 60% superwash merino wool, 25% mohair, 15% nylon, 4oz/112g = approx 560yd/504m per skein 2 skeins, Thistle

knitty BITS

Keeping It Up

● **The sock should stay in place nicely. If you have issues with the sock staying up above your knee, I suggest the following options:**

- Fold cuff over 1"/2.5cm, insert band of elastic, and sew shut.

- Thread fine elastic through a sewing needle and loosely sew spiraling rounds along the inside of the cuff. Be careful to only sew through inside stitches so the elastic doesn't show. Space the stitches about an inch apart so the cuff doesn't pucker.

- Wear the thigh highs with garters.

- Make knee socks instead. Work the pattern until just below the knee and bind off using the elastic bind-off method described.

SKILL LEVEL
Experienced

FINISHED MEASUREMENTS
Foot circumference 7 (7½, 8)"/18 (19, 20.5)cm (sizes Small [Medium, Large])

Leg length 13½"/34.5cm

Foot length 7¾(8½, 9¼)"/20 (21.5, 23.5)cm

MATERIALS AND TOOLS
Approx total: 500yd/450m of  fingering weight yarn, wool/ silk, in ice blue/green

Knitting needles: 2.25mm (size 1 U.S.) set of 4 double-pointed needles, 2 circular needles, or 1 long circular needle, *or size to obtain gauge*

Crochet hook: 0.6mm (size 14 U.S.)

Stitch markers, at least one should be removable

Approx 244 seed beads—size 8/0

Yarn needle

GAUGE
34 sts and 50 rows = 4"/10cm in Stockinette Stitch (knit every round)

Always take time to check your gauge.

Special Abbreviations
Place bead (B): With crochet hook, impale bead onto hook, insert hook into stitch loop where the bead will sit, making sure that the hook is facing you. Pull the stitch loop through the bead. Place the beaded stitch onto the right needle and proceed. In all cases, work stitch or decrease indicated before placing bead on stitch loop. For example, "sk2pB" would be worked as follows: Perform sk2p, place bead on stitch, place beaded stitch onto right needle and proceed.

Left leaning increase (LL): Insert left needle from back to front into stitch two rows below last stitch on right needle, lift onto left needle and knit into the back of the stitch.

Right leaning increase (LR): Insert right needle from back to front into stitch one row below first stitch on left needle, lift onto left needle and knit into the front of the stitch.

Afternoon Delight

There's only one thing better than beaded socks: beaded knee highs! Perfect for lounging, sashaying, and dancing, when you wear these socks, he'll have no choice but to treat you like the princess you are.

by SIVIA HARDING

(64, 68) sts is achieved. On last round 2, decrease 1 st somewhere in the round—59 (63, 67) sts.

FOOT

Round 1: K0 (1, 2), p2, k1 tbl, p2, work Lace pattern over 19 sts, p2, k1 tbl, p2, knit to end of round.

Repeat last round until the Sock measures 3¼"/8.5cm shorter than the length of your foot.

GUSSET

Round 1: K0 (1, 2), p2, k1 tbl, p2, work Lace pattern over 19 sts, p2, k1 tbl, p2, k1 (2, 3), LR, k28 (30, 32), LL, k1—61 (65, 69) sts.

Round 2: K0 (1, 2), p2, k1 tbl, p2, work Lace pattern over 19 sts, p2, k1 tbl, p2, knit to end of round.

Continue to increase 2 stitches every other round 9 more times—79 (83, 87) sts. Make a note of the last round worked of the Lace pattern. On last round 2, stop after 29 (31, 33) sts have been worked (for instep). Redistribute remaining stitches (for heel) onto one needle.

TOE

Using your chosen toe-up cast-on method, cast on 20 sts, or 10 sts on each of two needles. Place a removable stitch marker for beginning of round.

Round 1: Knit.

Toe Increases

Round 1 (Increase): *K1, LR, k8, LL, k1; repeat from * once more—22 sts.

Round 2: Knit.

Repeat last 2 rounds, working two additional stitches between increases on every round 2 until a total of 60

Turn Heel

Note: Work back and forth on heel stitches only.

Row 1 (RS): K39 (41, 43), w&t.

Row 2: P28 (30, 32), w&t.

Row 3: Knit to 1 st before wrapped st, w&t.

Row 4: Purl to 1 st before wrapped st, w&t.

Repeat last 2 rows until there are 5 wrapped stitches on each end; end with a WS row.

Next row: K20 (22, 24), pick up wraps on next 4 sts and knit them together with the sts they wrapped; for the last wrapped st, pick up wrap and knit these 2 sts together with the next unwrapped st (3 sts together), turn.

Next row: Sl 1 st as if to purl, p24 (26, 28), pick up wraps on next 4 sts and purl them together with the sts they wrapped; for the last wrapped st, pick up wrap and purl these 2 sts together with the next unwrapped st (3 sts together), turn.

HEEL FLAP

Continue to work back and forth on heel stitches for the heel flap.

Row 1 (RS): Sl 1 st as if to purl, k28 (30, 32), ssk, turn.

Row 2 (WS): Sl 1 st as if to purl, p28 (30, 32), p2tog, turn.

Repeat last 2 rows six more times, or until there are 2 sts left on both sides of the gap; end with a WS row.

LEG

Resume Working in the Round

With RS facing, knit to 1 st before the gap, ssk, k1. Beginning the next round, work across the instep sts continuing with the next pattern round of the Lace pattern as established; k1, k2tog, knit to 1 st before the gap, ssk—60 (64, 68) sts.

Next round: Work across the instep sts in pattern as established, k2tog, inc 1 (3, 5) sts evenly over remaining heel sts—60 (66, 72) sts.

Move beginning of round 4 (3, 2) sts to the left by knitting the first 4 (3, 2) sts of the round onto the last needle used. Place a marker to designate the new beginning of round.

Establish Pattern as follows:

Size Small only: *P1, work Lace pattern over 19 sts; repeat from * 2 more times.

Sizes Medium (Large) only: *P1 (2), k1 tbl, p1 (2), work Lace Pattern over 19 sts; repeat from * 2 more times.

Size Medium only: Switch position of first and second sts (i.e., work first st in manner previously used for second st, and vice versa) and 24th and 25th sts on the first round.

All sizes: Work in established pattern until sock measures 6"/15cm from top of heel.

lace pattern (worked in the round over 19 sts)

Round 1: K2, yo, ssk, k3, k2tog, yo, k1, yo, ssk, k3, k2tog, yo, k2.
Rounds 2, 4, 6, and 8: Knit.
Round 3: (Yo, ssk, k1) twice, k2tog, yo, k3, yo, ssk, (k1, k2tog, yo) twice.
Round 5: K1, yo, ssk, k1, yo, sk2pB, yo, k5, yo, sk2pB, yo, k1, k2tog, yo, k1.
Round 7: K2, yo, ssk, k2tog, yo, k7, yo, ssk, k2tog, yo, k2.
Round 9: K3, k2tog, k4, yo, k1B, yo, k4, ssk, k3.
Round 10: K2, k2tog, k4, yo, k3, yo, k4, ssk, k2.
Round 11: K1, k2tog, k4, yo, k5, yo, k4, ssk, k1.
Round 12: K2tog, k4, yo, k7, yo, k4, ssk.
Round 13: K3, k2tog, k4, yo, k1B, yo, k4, ssk, k3.
Round 14: K2, k2tog, k4, yo, k3, yo, k4, ssk, k2.
Round 15: K1, k2tog, k4, yo, k5, yo, k4, ssk, k1.
Round 16: K2tog, k4, yo, k7, yo, k4, ssk.
Round 17: Yo, ssk, k1, k2tog, yo, k9, yo, ssk, k1, k2tog, yo.
Rounds 18 and 20: Knit.
Round 19: K1, yo, sk2pB, yo, k11, yo, sk2pB, yo, k1.

Leg Increases

Size Small only:

Next round (Increase): *P1, m1p, work Lace pattern over 19 sts; repeat from * 2 more times—63 sts.

Next 9 rounds: *P2, work Lace pattern over 19 sts; repeat from * 2 more times.

Next round (Increase): *P1, m1k, p1, work Lace pattern over 19 sts; repeat from * 2 more times—66 sts.

Next 9 rounds: *P1, k1 tbl, p1, work Lace pattern over 19 sts; repeat from * 2 more times.

Next round (Increase): *P1, m1p, k1 tbl, m1p, p1, work Lace pattern over 19 sts; repeat from * 2 more times—72 sts.

Next round: *P2, k1 tbl, p2, work Lace pattern over 19 sts; repeat from * 2 more times.

Continue even as established until sock measures 12"/30.5cm from top of heel.

Sizes Medium (Large) only:

Next round (Increase): *P1 (2), k1 tbl, m1k, p1 (2), work Lace pattern over 19 sts; repeat from * 2 more times—69 (75) sts.

Next 9 rounds: *P1 (2), k2 tbl, p1 (2), work Lace pattern over 19 sts; repeat from * 2 more times.

Next round (Increase): *P1 (2), k1 tbl, m1p, k1 tbl, p1 (2), work Lace pattern over 19 sts; repeat from * 2 more times—72 (78) sts.

Next 9 rounds: *P1 (2), k1 tbl, p1, k1 tbl, p1 (2) work Lace pattern over 19 sts; repeat from * 2 more times.

Next round (Increase): *P1 (2), k1 tbl, m1p, p1, k1 tbl, p1 (2), work Lace pattern over 19 sts; repeat from * 2 more times—75 (81) sts.

Next 9 rounds: *P1 (2), k1 tbl, p2, k1 tbl, p1 (2), work Lace pattern over 19 sts; repeat from * 2 more times.

Next round (Increase): *P1 (2), k1 tbl, p1, m1k, p1, k1 tbl, p1 (2), work Lace pattern over 19 sts; repeat from * 2 more times—78 (84) sts.

Next round: *P1 (2), (k1 tbl, p1) twice, k1 tbl, p1 (2), work Lace pattern over 19 sts; repeat from * 2 more times.

Continue even as established until sock measures 12"/30.5cm from top of heel.

off the charts

lace

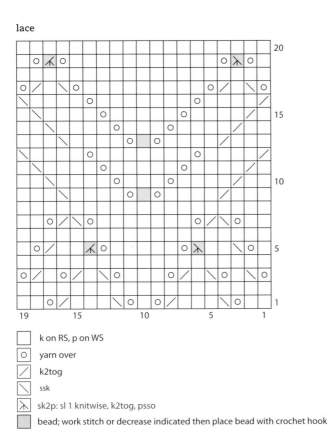

☐	k on RS, p on WS	
○	yarn over	
╱	k2tog	
╲	ssk	
人	sk2p: sl 1 knitwise, k2tog, psso	
▨	bead; work stitch or decrease indicated then place bead with crochet hook	

Ribbing and Bind Off

Size Medium only: Move start of round 1 stitch to the left by purling 1 stitch onto the last needle used. Place a new marker to designate new start of round.

All sizes:

Next 15 rounds: *K1 tbl, p1; repeat from * around.

FINISHING

Bind off using a stretchy sewn bind off. Weave in ends.

This project was knit with:

Sundara Yarn's Fingering Silky Merino, fingering weight, 50% silk/50% merino wool, 5.25oz/150g = approx 500yd/450m per hank
1 hank, robin's egg
Earth Faire's Galvanized Platinum Gold seed beads—size 8/0

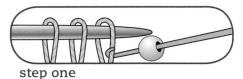

hooking beads

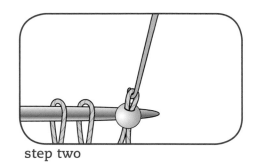

step one

step two

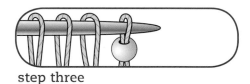

step three

Fleur Play

Does your significant other have trouble relinquishing control? Slip on these fancy fleur de coeur colorwork socks, and he'll tune everything else out.

CUFF

With B, cast on 60 sts. Distribute sts evenly over three needles (20 sts per needle). Place a stitch marker for beginning of round. Taking care not to twist sts, join to work in the round.

Round 1 (RS): *K2 with B, *p2 with A, bring A to the back, k2 with B; repeat from * to last 2 sts, p2 with A.

Repeat last round for 1¼"/3cm. Cut A and B, leaving long tails to weave in later.

LEG

With C and D, work chart 1, with one pattern repeat on each needle. Cut yarns C and D, leaving long tails to weave in later.

With E and B, work chart 1, with one pattern repeat on each needle. Cut yarns E and B, leaving long tails to weave in later.

With A and C, work chart 1, with one pattern repeat on each needle. Cut yarns A and C, leaving long tails to weave in later.

HEEL FLAP

Redistribute stitches so that the center (join) is in the middle of needle #1 with 15 stitches on either side of join (for a total of 30 heel stitches). The other 30 stitches should be held on needle #2 (for instep).

Note: The heel flap is worked in rows. Two rows are worked with the RS facing, and alternating colors. The next two rows are worked with the WS facing, and alternating colors.

Row 1 (RS): With RS facing, and working heel stitches, join A and knit across row.

Row 2 (RS): With RS facing, *sl 1 A st as if to purl, k1 with B; repeat from * across.

Row 3 (WS): With WS facing, *sl 1 B st as if to purl, p1 with A; repeat from * across.

Row 4 (WS): With WS facing, *p1 with B, sl 1 A st as if to purl; repeat from * across.

Row 5: With RS facing, *k1 with A, sl 1 B st as if to purl; repeat from * across.

Repeat rows 2–5 for a total of 29 rows, ending with row 4. Cut A and B, leaving long tails to weave in later.

by LINDSAY OBERMEYER

GUSSET

With RS facing and continuing with C, with one needle knit across heel stitches and with same needle pick up through back loop and knit (in effect, twisting the stitches) 15 sts along side of heel flap (needle #1); with another needle knit across instep sts (needle #2); with another needle pick up through back loop and knit 15 sts along opposite side of heel flap, then knit across 9 heel sts on needle #1 (needle #3). You should now have 24 sts on needle #1, 30 sts on needle #2, and 24 sts on needle #3.

Round 1:

Needle #1: *K1 with C, k1 with D; repeat from * to end.

Needle #2: Work 4 repeats of row 1 of chart 2.

Needle #3: *K1 with C, k1 with D; repeat from * to end.

Round 2:

Needle #1: Knit in established pattern to last 3 sts, k2tog, k1—23 sts.

Needle #2: Work 4 repeats of next row of chart 2.

Needle #3: K1, ssk, knit in established pattern to end—23 sts.

Round 3:

Needle #1: *K1 with C, k1 with D; repeat from * to end.

Needle #2: Work 4 repeats of next row of chart 2.

Needle #3: *K1 with C, k1 with D; repeat from * to end.

Repeat last 2 rounds until 60 sts remain (15 sts each on needles #1 and #3, and 30 sts on needle #2).

Note: Take care to maintain established stripe pattern when decreasing.

Turn Heel

Row 1 (RS): With RS facing and C, k17, ssk, k1, turn.

Row 2 (WS): Sl 1 as if to purl, p5, p2tog, p1, turn.

Row 3: Sl 1 as if to purl, purl to 1 st before gap, p2tog (1 st from each side of gap), p1, turn.

Row 4: Sl 1 as if to purl, knit to 1 st before gap, ssk (1 st from each side of gap), k1, turn.

Repeat last two rows until all heel stitches have been worked, ending with a WS row—18 sts.

chart 1 (first repeat)

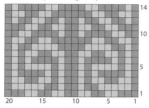

chart 1 (2nd repeat)

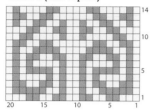

chart 1 (3rd repeat)

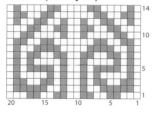

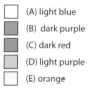

- ☐ (A) light blue
- ▨ (B) dark purple
- ▨ (C) dark red
- ▨ (D) light purple
- ☐ (E) orange

off the charts

chart 2

FOOT

Slip 2 sts at end of needle #1 to beginning of needle #2.

Slip 2 sts at beginning of needle #3 to end of needle #2.

You should now have 13 sts on needle #1, 34 sts on needle #2, and 13 sts on needle #3.

Continue in established pattern until piece measures 5½"/14cm (or 3"/7.5cm less than desired foot length) from heel flap, ending with needle #3. Cut C and D, leaving long tails to weave in later.

Slip 2 sts at beginning of needle #2 to end of needle #1.

Slip 2 sts at end of needle #2 to beginning of needle #3.

You should now have 15 sts on needle #1, 30 sts on needle #2, and 15 sts on needle #3.

TOE

Round 1: *K1 with B, k1 with A; repeat from * around.

Round 2: Maintain established stripe pattern.

Needle #1: Knit to last 3 sts, k2tog, k1—14 sts.

Needle #2: K1, ssk, knit to last 3 sts, K2tog, k1—28 sts.

Needle #3: K1, ssk, knit to end—14 sts.

Round 3: Maintain established stripe pattern and knit around.

Repeat last 2 rounds until 28 sts remain.

Repeat round 2 only until 12 sts remain.

Finish Toe

Knit sts from needle #1 onto needle #3. There should now be 6 sts each on needle #2 and needle #3. Cut yarn, leaving 18"/45.5cm tail on far end of needle #3, and leaving a shorter tail for other yarns, to weave in later. Use Kitchener Stitch to join the two sets of stitches.

FINISHING

Weave in ends. Block if desired.

This project was knit with:

Blue Sky Alpaca's Silk, sport weight, 50% alpaca/50% silk, 1.75oz/50g = approx 146yd/131m per ball
(A) 1 ball, #137 sapphire
(B) 1 ball, #128 plum
(C) 1 ball, #138 garnet
(D) 1 ball, #129 amethyst
(E) 1 ball, #126 brick

Chick Flick

Yeah, he pretends that it doesn't matter when Harry and Sally finally get together, but you know better—the big lug. A delicate lily stitch paired with a saucy scallop make the perfect double feature.

by MELANIE GIBBONS

SKILL LEVEL
Experienced

FINISHED MEASUREMENTS
Foot circumference
8½"/21.5cm

Leg length 7"/18cm

Foot length 8½"/21.5cm

MATERIALS AND TOOLS
Approx total: 370yd/333m
🔟 fingering weight yarn,
wool, in champagne

Knitting needles: 2mm
(size 0 U.S.) set of 5
double-pointed needles,
or size to obtain gauge

Stitch marker

Yarn needle

GAUGE
36 sts and 48 rows = 4"/10cm
in Stockinette Stitch (knit
every round)
*Always take time to check
your gauge.*

CUFF

Cast on 76 sts. Distribute the stitches evenly over four needles (19 sts per needle). Place a stitch marker for beginning of round. Taking care not to twist stitches, join to work in the round.

Knit 1 round.

Work 12 rounds in Scalloped Cuff pattern.

LEG

Work 72 rounds in Lily Stitch pattern.

Redistribute stitches as follows: Slip first st of needle #3 to end of needle #2. Place remaining 18 sts of needle #3 on needle #4 (for heel flap)—37 sts for heel flap (on needle #4), 39 sts for instep (on needles #1 and #2).

HEEL FLAP

Row 1: With WS of heel facing, sl 1, p36, turn.

Row 2 (RS): *Sl 1 as if to knit, k1; repeat from * to last st, k1.

Repeat last 2 rows until 38 rows have been worked.

Turn Heel

Row 1 (WS): Sl 1, p19, p2tog, p1, turn.

Row 2: Sl 1, k4, ssk, k1, turn.

Row 3: Sl 1, p5, p2tog, p1, turn.

Continue working in this manner, working one additional stitch before the decrease on each row, until 21 stitches remain; end with a RS row.

GUSSET

Redistribute stitches as follows: With RS of heel facing, divide heel sts placing 10 sts on needle #3 and 11 sts on needle #4; working yarn should be at the end of the sts on needle #4; with needle #4 pick up and knit 20 sts along side of heel flap; work across needles #1 and #2 in Lily Stitch pattern; with spare needle, pick up and knit 20 sts along opposite side of heel flap, k across 10 sts held on needle #3; knit to last 3 sts on needle #4, k2tog, k1—99 sts (19 sts on needle #1, 20 sts on needle #2, 30 sts each on needle #3 and needle #4).

Note: The last stitch on needle #2 will be purled every round until toe shaping begins

Round 2:

Needles #1 and #2: Work in established pattern.

Needles #3 and #4: Knit.

Round 3:

Needles #1 and #2: Work in established pattern.

Needle #3: K1, ssk, k to end—29 sts.

Needle #4: K to last 3 sts, k2tog, k1—29 sts.

scalloped cuff stitch pattern (multiples of 19 sts)

Round 1: *K1, yo, k1, yo, k1, (ssk) twice, k1, p1, k2tog, yo, p1, k1, (k2tog) twice, k1, yo, k1, yo; repeat from * around.

Round 2: *K8, p1, yo, ssk, p1, k7; repeat from * around.

Round 3: *P9, k2tog, yo, p8; repeat from * around.

Round 4: Repeat round 2.

Repeat rounds 1–4 for Scalloped Cuff pattern.

lily stitch pattern (multiples of 38 sts)

Round 1: *P1, yo, k2, ssk, k3, p1, k2tog, yo, p1, yo, k2, ssk, k3, p1, k3, k2tog, k2, yo, p1, k2tog, yo, p1, k3, k2tog, k2, yo; repeat from * around.

Round 2: *P1, k1, yo, k2, ssk, k2, p1, yo, ssk, p1, k1, yo, k2, ssk, k2, p1, k2, k2tog, k2, yo, k1, p1, yo, ssk, p1, k2, k2tog, k2, yo, k1; repeat from * around.

Round 3: *P1, k2, yo, k2, ssk, k1, p1, k2tog, yo, p1, k2, yo, k2, ssk, k1, p1, k1, k2tog, k2, yo, k2, p1, k2tog, yo, p1, k1, k2tog, k2, yo, k2; repeat from * around.

Round 4: *P1, k3, yo, k2, ssk, p1, yo, ssk, p1, k3, yo, k2, ssk, p1, k2tog, k2, yo, k3, p1, yo, ssk, p1, k2tog, k2, yo, k3; repeat from * around.

Round 5: *P1, k4, yo, ssk, k1, p1, k2tog, yo, p1, k4, yo, ssk, k1, p1, k1, k2tog, yo, k4, p1, k2tog, yo, p1, k1, k2tog, yo, k4; repeat from * around.

Round 6: *P1, k5, yo, k2tog, p1, yo, ssk, p1, k5, yo, k2tog, p1, ssk, yo, k5, p1, yo, ssk, p1, ssk, yo, k5; repeat from * around.

Rounds 7–12: Repeat rounds 1–6.

Round 13: *P1, k3, k2tog, k2, yo, p1, k2tog, yo, p1, k3, k2tog, k2, yo, p1, yo, k2, ssk, k3, p1, k2tog, yo, p1, yo, k2, ssk, k3; repeat from * around.

Round 14: *P1, k2, k2tog, k2, yo, k1, p1, yo, ssk, p1, k2, k2tog, k2, yo, k1, p1, k1, yo, k2, ssk, k2, p1, yo, ssk, p1, k1, yo, k2, ssk, k2; repeat from * around.

Round 15: *P1, k1, k2tog, k2, yo, k2, p1, k2tog, yo, p1, k1, k2tog, k2, yo, k2, p1, k2, yo, k2, ssk, k1, p1, k2tog, yo, p1, k2, yo, k2, ssk, k1; repeat from * around.

Round 16: *P1, k2tog, k2, yo, k3, p1, yo, ssk, p1, k2tog, k2, yo, k3, p1, k3, yo, k2, ssk, p1, yo, ssk, p1, k3, yo, k2, ssk; repeat from * around.

Round 17: *P1, k1, k2tog, yo, k4, p1, k2tog, yo, p1, k1, k2tog, yo, k4, p1, k4, yo, ssk, k1, p1, k2tog, yo, p1, k4, yo, ssk, k1; repeat from * around.

Round 18: *P1, ssk, yo, k5, p1, yo, ssk, p1, ssk, yo, k5, p1, k5, yo, k2tog, p1, yo, ssk, p1, k5, yo, k2tog; repeat from * around.

Rounds 19–24: Repeat rounds 13–18.

Repeat rounds 1–24 for Lily Stitch pattern.

Repeat last 2 rounds until needles #3 and #4 have 18 sts each—75 sts (39 sts on needles #1 and #2 for instep, 36 sts on needles #3 and #4 for sole).

Work rounds in established pattern, without further decreasing, until a total of 72 rounds have been worked following the heel flap, or until foot measures 2"/5cm less than desired total foot length.

Shape Toe

Slip first st of needle #2 to end of needle #1 (needle #1 now holds 20 sts).

Round 1:

Needle #1: K1, ssk, k7, k2tog, k6, k2tog—17 sts.

Needle #2: K7, k2tog, k7, k2tog, k1—17 sts.

Needle #3: K1, ssk, k15—17 sts.

Needle #4: K15, k2tog, k1—17 sts.

Round 2: Knit.

Round 3:

Needle #1: K1, ssk, k to end.

Needle #2: K to last 3 sts, k2tog, k1.

Needle #3: K1, ssk, k to end.

Needle #4: K to last 3 sts, k2tog, k1.

Repeat last 2 rounds until 9 sts remain on each needle—36 sts total.

Repeat round 3 only 4 more times—20 sts total (5 sts on each needle).

lily stitch

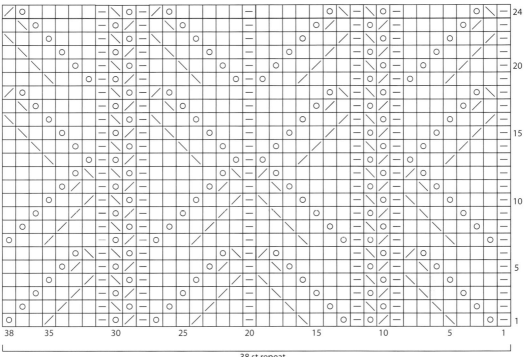

38 st repeat

Finish Toe

Slip stitches from needle #1 onto needle #2, and slip stitches from needle #3 onto needle #4. Cut yarn, leaving an 8"/20.5cm tail. Use Kitchener Stitch to sew the two sets of stitches together.

FINISHING

Weave in ends.

This project was knit with:

Louet's Gems, fingering weight, 100% merino wool, 1.75oz/50g = approx 185yd/167m per skein 2 skeins, #01 champagne

scalloped cuff stitch

						k on RS, p on WS
					—	p on RS, k on WS
					○	yarn over
					/	k2tog
					\	ssk

19 st repeat

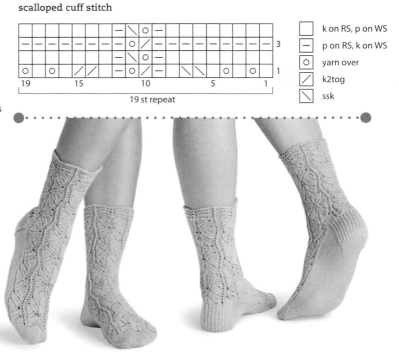

Last of the Red Hot Lovers

by JANINE LE CRAS

TOE

Cast on 8 sts onto one
double-pointed needle.
Knit one row. With a second
double-pointed needle, pick
up and k8 sts along the cast-
on edge. You should now have
two needles, parallel to each
other, with 8 stitches on each.
Place a marker to indicate the
beginning of the round.

Toe Increases
Round 1: *K1, m1, knit to
last st on needle, m1, k1;
repeat from * across second
needle—20 sts.

Round 2: Knit.

Repeat last 2 rounds eleven
more times—64 sts.

Arrange the stitches on four
double-pointed needles as
follows: Place 17 sts each on
needles #1 and #2, place 15
sts each on needles #3 and
#4.

Next round:

Needles #1 and #2: Work
row 1 of chart 1 across;

Needles #3 and #4: Knit.

Next round:

Needles #1 and #2: Work
next row of chart across;

Needles #3 and #4: Knit.

Repeat last round until all rows
of chart have been completed.
Beginning with row 3 of chart
for each repeat, repeat last
round until chart 1 has been
completed one more time.

**Note: When working repeats
of chart 1, always begin each
repeat at row 3 from here
on.**

Shape Gusset
Round 1:

Needles #1 and #2: Work in
established pattern across;

Needle #3: K1, m1, knit to
end —16 sts;

Needle #4: Knit to last st,
m1, k1—16 sts (66 sts total).

Round 2:

Needles #1 and #2: Work in
established pattern across;

Needles #3 and #4: Knit.

Repeat last 2 rounds 14 more
times. You should have 30 sts

Let the games begin. While competition may be running high, we're pretty sure these red-hot socks, with both heart and lover's knot cable patterns, will give you the advantage.

each on needles #3 and #4. Work even in established pattern until you have completed row 15 of chart 1.

Next round:

Needles #1 and #2: Work row 16 of chart 1; slip all of these stitches to a stitch holder or waste yarn (for instep);

Needle #3 and #4: Do not work at this time, these are the heel stitches.

HEEL

Note: The heel is worked back and forth over the 60 stitches on needles #3 and #4 only.

Row 1 (RS): k33, ssk, k1, turn.

Row 2 (WS): Sl 1, p7, p2tog, p1, turn.

Row 3: Sl 1, k8, ssk, k1, turn.

Row 4: Sl 1, p9, p2tog, p1, turn.

Continue as established, working one more stitch before the decrease on each row, until you have 17 sts left on each needle.

Next row (RS): Sl 1, (k2tog, k8) twice, ssk, k8, ssk, k1, do not turn. You should now have 60 stitches on needles #3 and #4 only (arrange them so that you have 15 sts on each needle).

Slip instep stitches back onto needles #1 and #2 (17 sts on each needle).

Next round:

Needles #1 and #2: Continue working chart 1 as established;

Needles #3 and #4: Work first row of chart 2 across.

Next round:

Needles #1 and #2: Continue working chart 1 as established;

Needles #3 and #4: Work next row of chart 2 across.

Next round: Repeat last round to complete current repetition of both charts.

LEG

Round 1: Starting on needle 1, at stitch 28 on chart 3, work row 1 of chart 3.

Round 2: Work next row of chart 3.

Repeat last round until all rows of chart 3 have been completed four times. Then repeat last round until rows 1–3 of chart 3 have been completed.

CUFF

Using stitches of last round as a guide, work in K2, p2 Rib for 12 rounds. Cast off all stitches loosely.

FINISHING

Weave in ends. Block if desired.

This project was knit with:

Cherry Tree Hill Yarn's Supersock, fingering weight, 100% wool, 3.5oz/100g = approx 420yd/378m per skein 1 skein, Cherry

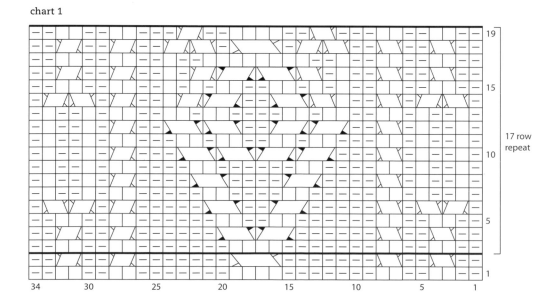

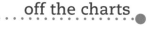

chart 1

chart 2

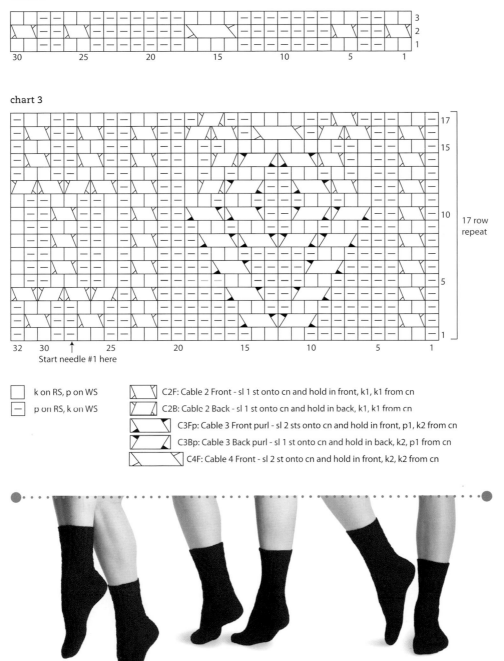

chart 3

17 row repeat

Start needle #1 here

	k on RS, p on WS
−	p on RS, k on WS

C2F: Cable 2 Front - sl 1 st onto cn and hold in front, k1, k1 from cn

C2B: Cable 2 Back - sl 1 st onto cn and hold in back, k1, k1 from cn

C3Fp: Cable 3 Front purl - sl 2 sts onto cn and hold in front, p1, k2 from cn

C3Bp: Cable 3 Back purl - sl 1 st onto cn and hold in back, k2, p1 from cn

C4F: Cable 4 Front - sl 2 st onto cn and hold in front, k2, k2 from cn

Blue Crush

The secret's out: there's no use denying your feelings for lace socks, especially the blue floral-inspired kind.

SKILL LEVEL
Experienced

FINISHED MEASUREMENTS
Foot circumference 7½"/19cm

Leg length 8½"/21.5cm

Foot length 9½"/24cm

MATERIALS AND TOOLS
Approx total: 400yd/360m of
🧶 fingering weight yarn,
wool, in variegated blue-
purple

Knitting needles: 2.25mm
(size 1 U.S.) two circular
needles 12"/30cm long,
and 2.25mm (size 1 U.S.)
set of 4 or 5 double-
pointed needles, *or size to
obtain gauge*

Stitch markers

Yarn needle

GAUGE
32 sts and 44 rows = 4"/10cm
in Stockinette Stitch (knit
every round)

*Always take time to check
your gauge.*

by JOLENE MOSLEY

CUFF

With both circular needles, cast on 60 sts. Place a stitch marker for beginning of round. Taking care not to twist stitches, join to work in the round.

Work 12 rounds in Ribbing.

LEG

Work 70 rounds in Leg Lace pattern (or to desired leg length). On last round, work 6 more sts following the beginning of round marker.

HEEL FLAP

Work back and forth over next 30 sts only (for heel). Hold remaining 30 sts on a circular needle (for instep).

Row 1 (RS): With double-pointed needle, sl 1, k29, turn.

Continue to work on heel flap stitches only, with 2 double-pointed needles.

Row 2 (WS): Sl 1 as if to purl, p29, turn.

Repeat last 2 rows 14 more times (for a total of 30 rows).

Turn Heel

Row 1 (RS): Sl 1, k16, k2tog, k1, turn.

Row 2: Sl 1, p5, p2tog, p1, turn.

Row 3: Sl 1, k6, k2tog, k1, turn.

Row 4: Sl 1, p7, p2tog, p1, turn.

Continue working in this manner working one additional stitch before the decrease on each row, until 18 stitches remain; end with a WS row.

foot lace pattern (worked over 30 sts)

Rows 1, 3, 5, 7, 9, 11, and 13: Knit.

Row 2: K7, yo, k4, k2tog, yo, s2kp2, yo, ssk, k4, yo, k8.

Row 4: K8, yo, k2, k3tog, yo, k3, yo, sk2p, k2, yo, k9.

Row 6: K3, yo, sk2p, yo, k3, yo, k1, k2tog, yo, k1, s2kp2, k1, yo, ssk, k1, yo, k3, yo, sk2p, yo, k4.

Row 8: K4, yo, k2tog, k4, yo, k2tog, yo, k1, s2kp2, k1, yo, ssk, yo, k5, yo, k2tog, k4.

Row 10: K8, k2tog, yo, k1, yo, k2, s2kp2, k2, yo, k1, yo, ssk, k9.

Row 12: K7, k2tog, yo, k3, yo, k1, s2kp2, k1, yo, k3, yo, ssk, k8.

Row 14: K6, k2tog, yo, k5, yo, s2kp2, yo, k5, yo, ssk, k7.

Repeat rows 1–14 for Foot Lace pattern.

leg lace pattern (worked over 60 sts)

Rounds 1, 3, 5, 7, 9, 11, and 13: Knit

Round 2: *K3, yo, k4, k2tog, yo, s2kp2, yo, ssk, k4, yo, k2; repeat from * 2 more times.

Round 4: *K4, yo, k2, k3tog, yo, k3, yo, sk2p, k2, yo, k3; repeat from * 2 more times.

Round 6: Skp, yo, k3, yo, k1, k2tog, yo, k1, s2kp2, k1, yo, ssk, k1, yo, k3, yo, sk2p, yo, k3, yo, k1, k2tog, yo, k1, s2kp2, k1, yo, ssk, k1, yo, k3, yo, sk2p, yo, k3, yo, k1, k2tog, yo, k1, s2kp2, k1, yo, ssk, k1, yo, k2, k2tog, yo.

Round 8: *Yo, k2tog, k4, yo, k2tog, yo, k1, s2kp2, k1, yo, ssk, yo, k5; repeat from * 2 more times.

Round 10: *K4, k2tog, yo, k1, yo, k2, s2kp2, k2, yo, k1, yo, ssk, k3; repeat from * 2 more times.

Round 12: *K3, k2tog, yo, k3, yo, k1, s2kp2, k1, yo, k3, yo, ssk, k2; repeat from * 2 more times.

Round 14: *K2, k2tog, yo, k5, yo, s2kp2, yo, k5, yo, ssk, k1; repeat from * 2 more times.

Repeat rounds 1–14 for Leg Lace pattern.

ribbing

Round 1: *K1, (p2, k2) twice, p1, k1, p1, (k2, p2) twice; repeat from * around.

Repeat round 1 for Ribbing.

forming), place a marker; begin working Foot Lace pattern and work across instep sts, place a marker; pick up and knit a st in the gap at the base of the heel flap, pick up and knit 15 sts along the other side of the heel flap—80 sts.

Round 2: Knit sts of sole, continue in Foot Lace pattern across instep.

Round 3: Knit to 3 sts before marker, k2tog, k1, continue in Foot Lace pattern across instep to next marker, k1, ssk, k to end—78 sts.

Repeat last 2 rounds until 60 sts remain on needle.

Continue to work the instep in Foot Lace pattern and the sole in Stockinette Stitch until the foot measures 2"/5cm less than desired total foot length.

Shape Toe
Round 1: K1, k2tog, k to 3 sts before marker, ssk, k2, k2tog, k to 3 sts before next marker, ssk, k1—56 sts.

Round 2: Knit.

Repeat last 2 rounds until 28 sts remain. Change to double-pointed needles when there are too few stitches to manage on the circular needles.

Finishing Toe
Cut yarn leaving a 30"/76cm tail. Redistribute stitches placing one-half (14 sts) of remaining stitches on each of two needles. Use Kitchener Stitch to sew the two sets of stitches together.

FINISHING
Sew small opening at top of cuff using Kitchener Stitch. Weave in ends.

This project was knit with:

C*eye*ber Fiber's, fingering weight, 80% superwash merino wool, 20% nylon, 4oz/113g = approx 435yd/392m per skein 1 skein, custom colorway

GUSSET
Return to working with both circular needles.

Round 1: Knit to end of heel sts, pick up and knit 15 sts along the side of the heel flap; pick up and knit a st in the gap at the base of the heel flap (to prevent a hole from

29%
listen to audio books while knitting, 22% prefer silence, and 17% rock out to rock music.

foot lace

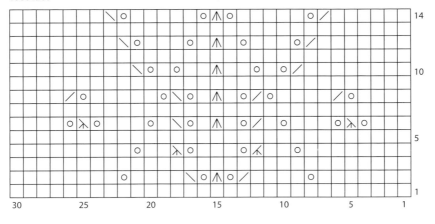

leg lace

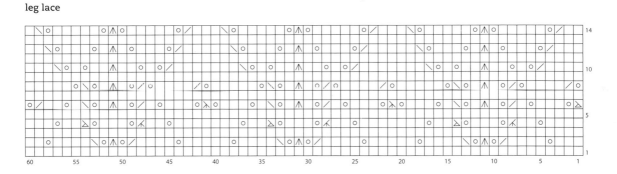

	k on RS, p on WS		k3tog
−	p on RS, k on WS		skp
o	yarn over		s2kp2: sl 2 as if to k2tog, k1, p2sso
/	k2tog		sk2p: sl 1 knitwise, k2tog, psso
\	ssk		

Lotus

If there's ever a sock to become "one" with, this is it. The scalloped cuff makes it sheer nirvana.

by ADRIENNE FONG

SKILL LEVEL
Intermediate

FINISHED MEASUREMENTS
Foot circumference 7½"/19cm

Leg length 6"/15cm

Foot length 9"/23cm

MATERIALS AND TOOLS
Approx total: 360yd/324m of
🧶 sock weight yarn, wool,
in plum

Knitting needles: 2.5mm
(size 1½ U.S.) 2 sets of 5
double-pointed needles,
or 1 to 2 pairs of circular
needles, *or size to obtain
gauge*

Waste yarn

Stitch markers

Stitch holder

Yarn needle

GAUGE
32 sts and 48 rows = 4"/10cm
in Stockinette Stitch (knit
every round)

*Always take time to check
your gauge.*

HEMMED PICOT CUFF

Using waste yarn and provisional cast-on method of your choice, cast on 68 sts. Place a stitch marker for beginning of round. Taking care not to twist stitches, change to project yarn, and join to work in the round.

Rounds 1–4: Knit.

Round 5 (fold line): *Yo, k2tog; repeat from * around.

Rounds 6–9: Knit.

Remove waste yarn from provisional cast on, and place stitches onto a spare set of needles. Fold at round 5 so WS are facing each other.

Hemming round: *Knit together one stitch from working needle and one stitch from provisional cast on; repeat from * around—68 sts.

Increase round: [K7, kfb, k8, p1] 4 times—72 sts.

LEG

Work rounds 2–28 of Leg Lace pattern. Work rounds 1–28 of Leg Lace pattern, then work rounds 1–7 of pattern once more.

Tip: For smaller yo's in rounds 19 and 27, skip the yo's, then pick up and knit the yarn between the stitches on next round.

Redistribute stitches as follows: Work 36 sts in Leg Lace pattern as established; place marker (for beginning of instep), work 35 sts in Leg Lace pattern as established; place marker (for beginning of heel flap), leave last st as positioned; this establishes the new beginning of the round and the beginning of the heel flap—35 instep sts and 37 heel sts.

Heel is worked back and forth over 37 heel sts only. Place 35 instep sts on a holder.

HEEL FLAP

Work rows 1–6 of Decorative Heel pattern. Repeat rows 3–6 of Decorative Heel pattern three times.

Decrease row (RS): K4, ssk, k3, p1, k3, k2tog, k3, p1, k3, ssk, k3, p1, k3, k2tog, k4—33 sts.

Row 1 (WS): P8, k1, p7, k1, p7, k1, p8.

Row 2: K8, p1, k7, p1, k7, p1, k8

Repeat rows 1 and 2 until heel flap measures 2⅜"/6cm (or desired length). End on row 2.

Turn Heel

Row 1 (WS): Sl 1, p19, p2tog, p1, turn.

Row 2: Sl 1, k8, ssk, k1, turn.

Row 3: Sl 1, p9, p2tog, p1, turn.

Row 4: Sl 1, k10, ssk, k1, turn.

Continue working in this manner, working one additional stitch before the decrease on each row, until all heel sts have been worked and 21 stitches remain. Do not turn.

leg lace pattern (multiples of 18 sts)

Rounds 1 and 2: *K8, p1; repeat from * around.

Round 3: *Yo, k3, ssk, k3, p1, k3, k2tog, k3, yo, p1; repeat from * around.

Round 4: *K1, yo, k3, ssk, k2, p1, k2, k2tog, k3, yo, k1, p1; repeat from * around.

Round 5: *K2, yo, k3, ssk, k1, p1, k1, k2tog, k3, yo, k2, p1; repeat from * around.

Round 6: *K3, yo, k3, ssk, p1, k2tog, k3, yo, k3, p1; repeat from * around.

Round 7: *Yo, k3, ssk, k3, p1, k3, k2tog, k3, yo, p1; repeat from * around.

Round 8: *K1, yo, k3, ssk, k2, p1, k2, k2tog, k3, yo, k1, p1; repeat from * around.

Round 9: *K2, yo, k3, ssk, k1, p1, k1, k2tog, k3, yo, k2, p1; repeat from * around.

Round 10: *K3, yo, k3, ssk, p1, k2tog, k3, yo, k3, p1; repeat from * around.

Round 11: *Yo, k3, ssk, k3, p1, k3, k2tog, k3, yo, p1; repeat from * around.

Round 12: *K1, yo, k3, ssk, k2, p1, k2, k2tog, k3, yo, k1, p1; repeat from * around.

Round 13: *K2, yo, k3, ssk, k1, p1, k1, k2tog, k3, yo, k2, p1; repeat from * around.

Round 14: *K3, yo, k3, ssk, p1, k2tog, k3, yo, k3, p1; repeat from * around.

Rounds 15–17: *K8, p1; repeat from * around.

Round 18: Purl.

Round 19: *[Yo, ssk] 4 times, p1, [k2tog, yo] 4 times, p1; repeat from * around.

Round 20: Purl.

Rounds 21 and 22: *K8, p1; repeat from * around.

Round 23: Yo, k1, yo, k1, yo, [ssk] 3 times, p1, [k2tog] 3 times, yo, k1, yo, k1, yo, p1; repeat from * around.

Rounds 24 and 25: *K8, p1; repeat from * around.

Round 26: Purl.

Rounds 27 and 28: Repeat rounds 19 and 20.

Repeat rounds 1–28 for Leg Lace pattern.

toe pattern stitch (worked over center 19 instep sts)

Round 1: P1, k3, k2tog, k3, yo, p1, yo, k3, ssk, k3, p1.
Round 2: P1, k2, k2tog, k3, yo, k1, p1, k1, yo, k3, ssk, k2, p1.
Round 3: P1, k1, k2tog, k3, yo, k2, p1, k2, yo, k3, ssk, k1, p1.
Round 4: P1, k2tog, k3, yo, k3, p1, k3, yo, k3, ssk, p1.
Round 5: K4, k2tog, k3, yo, p1, yo, k3, ssk, k4.

decorative heel pattern stitch (worked over 37 sts)

Row 1 (RS): K3, yo, k3, ssk, k1, p1, k1, k2tog, k3, yo, k2, p1, k2, yo, k3, ssk, k1, p1, k1, k2tog, k3, yo, k3.
Row 2: P4, yo, p3, ssp, k1, p2tog, p3, yo, p3, k1, p3, yo, p3, ssp, k1, p2tog, p3, yo, p4.
Row 3: K9, p1, k3, ssk, k3, yo, p1, yo, k3, k2tog, k3, p1, k9.
Row 4: P2, yo, p3, ssp, p2, k1, p2, p2tog, p3, yo, p1, k1, p1, yo, p3, ssp, p2, k1, p2, p2tog, p3, yo, p2.
Row 5: K3, yo, k3, ssk, k1, p1, k1, k2tog, k3, yo, k2, p1, k2, yo, k3, ssk, k1, p1, k1, k2tog, k3, yo, k3.
Row 6: P4, yo, p3, ssp, k1, p2tog, p3, yo, p3, k1, p3, yo, p3, ssp, k1, p2tog, p3, yo, p4.
Repeat rows 3–6 for Decorative Heel pattern.

Pick-up round: With RS of heel facing, pick up and knit 19 sts along side of heel flap, place marker (for gusset); continue in Leg Lace pattern as established, k35 instep sts, place marker (for gusset); pick up and knit 19 sts along opposite side of heel flap; k10 sts and place marker (for beginning of round)—94 sts (35 instep sts and 59 gusset and sole sts).

Note: The beginning of the round is now at the middle of the heel flap.

Tip: If you worked a longer or shorter heel flap, pick up and knit 8 sts for every inch/2.5cm along each side of heel flap.

Shape Gusset
Round 1: Knit to last st before gusset marker, p1; k35 instep sts in pattern as established; sl marker, p1, k to end.

Round 2 (decrease round): Knit to last 3 sts before gusset marker, k2tog, p1; k35 instep sts in pattern as established; sl marker, p1, ssk, k to end—35 instep sts and 57 gusset and sole sts.

Repeat last 2 rounds until 33 sts remain on the sole—35 instep sts and 33 sole sts.

Work rounds as established until foot measures 2"/5cm less than desired foot length. End on round 2, 6, 10, or 14 of Leg Lace pattern. If foot is shorter than desired, work rounds 3–6 only of Leg Lace pattern as established across instep, work sole sts even as established until foot is correct length, ending on round 6. Do not remove gusset markers; they now serve as instep markers.

Shape Toe
Round 1 (set-up): Knit to first instep marker, sl marker, k3, ssk, k3; work Toe pattern over 19 sts; k3, k2tog, k3, sl marker, k to end—33 instep sts and 33 sole sts.

Note: Toe pattern stitch is worked once only. Keep 19 center instep sts in Toe pattern until 5 rounds are completed. Then work instep sts in St st (k every round).

Round 2 (decrease): Knit to last 3 sts before first instep marker, k2tog, k1; sl marker, k1, ssk, k in pattern as established across to last 3 sts before second marker, k2tog, k1, sl marker; k1, ssk, k to end—31 instep sts and 31 sole sts.

Rounds 3–5: Knit to instep marker; sl marker, k in pattern as established across to second marker, sl marker, k to end.

Round 6 (decrease): Repeat round 2—29 instep sts and 29 sole sts.

Rounds 7 and 8: Repeat round 3.

Rounds 9–11: Repeat rounds 6–8—27 instep sts and 27 sole sts.

Round 12 (decrease): Repeat round 2—25 instep sts and 25 sole sts.

Round 13: Repeat round 3.

Rounds 14–17: Repeat rounds 12 and 13 twice—21 instep sts and 21 sole sts.

Rounds 18–22: Repeat round 2 five more times—11 instep sts and 11 sole sts.

Cut yarn, leaving an 18"/45.5cm tail (to weave toe sts together).

Finish Toe
Place instep stitches on one needle and sole stitches on another and hold needles parallel. Use Kitchener Stitch to sew the two sets of stitches together.

FINISHING
Weave in ends.

This project was knit with:

Claudia's Hand Painted Yarns, sock weight, 100% merino wool, 1.75oz/50g = approx 175yd/158m per skein 3 skeins, colorway "Just Plum"

Credit: Leg Lace pattern was adapted from pattern #143 in *Knitting Patterns Book 250* by Shida Hitomi.

toe chart

leg chart

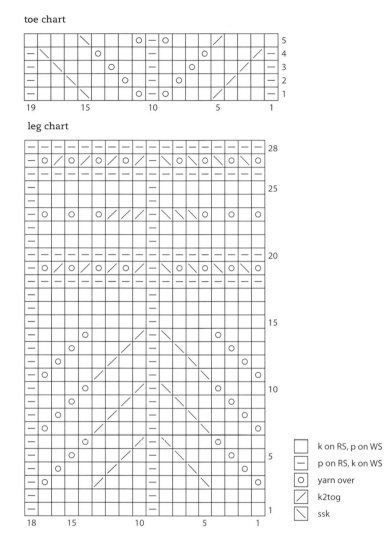

k on RS, p on WS
p on RS, k on WS
yarn over
k2tog
ssk

decorative heel chart

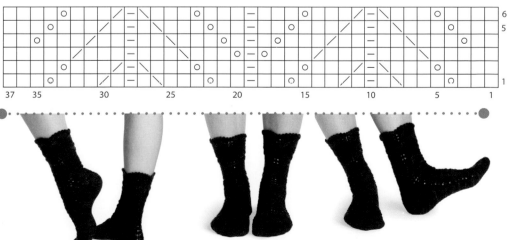

127

SKILL LEVEL
Intermediate

FINISHED MEASUREMENTS
Foot circumference 9½ (12)"/24 (30.5)cm

Leg length 9½ (10½)"/24 (27)cm

Foot length 8½ (10)"/21.5 (25.5)cm

MATERIALS AND TOOLS
Approx total: 420yd/378m of 🔟 fingering weight yarn, wool, in burgundy

Knitting needles: 2.5mm (size 1½ U.S.) 1 circular needle 32"/81.5cm long, *or size to obtain gauge*

Stitch marker

Cable needle

Stitch holder

Yarn needle

GAUGE
27 sts and 46 rows = 4"/10cm in Diagonal Lace pattern

Always take time to check your gauge.

Note:

The following instructions are written for socks worked using the magic loop technique.

Special Abbreviations
Right Diagonal Lace (RD): *K2tog, yo; repeat from *.

Left Diagonal Lace (LD): *Yo, ssk; repeat from *.

Warm Up Socks

Well, somebody has to keep count! Whip your honey into shape with these fine lace corset socks.

by SAUNIELL CONNALLY

TOE

Using Figure-8, Turkish, or preferred cast-on method, cast on 32 sts, divided into two sections of 16 sts each.

Round 1: K16 (front sts), slide needles, k16 (back sts).

Round 2: *K1, inc 1, work to last st on needle, inc 1, k1; repeat from * on back sts.

Repeat last 2 rounds until there are 32 (40) sts in each section.

Knit 2 rounds.

FOOT

Next round (pattern round 1): On front, work RD 5 (7) times, k2, p1, C4B, k2, p1, k2, work LD 5 (7) times; on back, knit all sts.

Next round (pattern round 2): K12 (16), p1, k6, p1, knit to end of round.

Next round (pattern round 3): On front, k1, RD 5 (7) times, k1, p1, k2, C4F, p1, k1, LD 5 (7) times, k1; on back, knit all sts.

Next round (pattern round 4): Repeat pattern round 2.

Repeat the last 4 rounds 16 (19) more times. On pattern round 4 of the last repeat, work only the front sts. The back sts will be worked when shaping the heel.

Shape Heel
Note: To shape heel, short rows are worked back and forth on back stitches only.

Begin short row shaping

Row 1 (RS): K31 (39), w&t.

Row 2 (WS): P30 (38), w&t.

Row 3: Knit to 1 st before wrapped st, w&t.

Row 4: Purl to 1 st before wrapped st, w&t.

Repeat last 2 rows until there are 14 (18) unwrapped sts, ending with a WS row.

Next row (RS): Knit to the nearest wrapped st, knit the wrapped st; pick up the wrap with the left needle and then wrap the next 2 sts on the left needle (the picked up wrap st and the next st); turn.

Next row (WS): Purl to the nearest wrapped st, purl the wrapped st; pick up the wrap with the left needle and then wrap the 2 sts on the left needle; turn.

Next row: Knit to the 2 wrapped sts, k3tog working through the wrap and the 2 sts that it was wrapping; pick up the wrap with the left needle and then wrap the next two sts on the left needle; turn.

Next row: Purl to the 2 wrapped sts, p3tog tbl through the wrap and the 2 sts that it was wrapping; pick up the wrap with the left needle and then wrap the next two sts on the left needle; turn.

Repeat last 2 rows until the last stitch on WS is wrapped.

Next row (RS): Knit to the last 2 wrapped sts, k3tog working through the wrap and the 2 sts that it was wrapping; pick up the wrap with the left needle; with the first st of the front sts, k2tog through st and wrap; continue working 30 (38) sts of pattern round 1; with last st on front and the lowermost wrap on the first st on back, k2tog tbl; on back, k3tog through wrap and 2 sts it was wrapping, knit to end of round.

Work pattern rounds 2–4.

LEG

Next round (leg pattern round 1): On front, work RD 5 (7) times, k2, p1, C4B, k2, p1, k2, work LD 5 (7) times; on back, k1, RD 7 (9) times, k2, LD 7 (9) times, k1.

Next round (leg pattern round 2): Knit 12 (16) sts, p1, k6, p1, knit to end of round.

Next round (leg pattern round 3): On front, k1, RD 5 (7) times, k1, p1, k2, C4F, p1, k1, LD 5 (7) times, k1; on back, RD 7 (9) times, k4, LD 7 (9) times, k1.

Next round (leg pattern round 4): Repeat pattern round 2.

Repeat last 4 rounds 19 (21) more times.

Next round: Knit.

CUFF

Work in K1, p1 Rib for 8 rounds. Bind off loosely.

FINISHING

Weave in ends. Block if desired.

This project was knit with:

Cherry Tree Hill's Super-sock solids, fingering weight, 100% merino wool, 4oz/113g = approx 420yd/378m per ball 1 ball, Burgundy

knitty BITS

I See Sock People

You've seen them around: knitters who can't look you in the face because they're staring uncontrollably at your socks. These so-called Sock People are invading online chat rooms and social networking sites across the world. How do you know when you've crossed to the dark side and become a full-fledged member of the Sock People?

- You agree with the following statement: "Sock yarn does not count as stash."
- You're steadily, and proudly, phasing out your commercial socks.
- You buy shoes based on their sock-showing-off potential.

Main Squeeze

Everything's better with a squeezebox! Don these lovely show stoppers—featuring three-dimensional triangles and plenty of fun colors—for your next performance. But we know the real reason daddy never sleeps at night....

by KATHRYN ALEXANDER

SKILL LEVEL
Intermediate

FINISHED MEASUREMENTS
Foot circumference 8"/20.5cm

Leg length 10"/25.5cm

Foot length custom

MATERIALS AND TOOLS
Approx total: 455yd/416m of (3) DK weight yarn, wool

Color A: 42yd/38m of (3) DK weight yarn, wool, in lavender

Color B: 42yd/38m of (3) DK weight yarn, wool, in periwinkle

Color C: 38yd/34m of (3) DK weight yarn, wool, in green

Color D: 38yd/34m of (3) DK weight yarn, wool, in aqua

Color E: 50yd/45m of (3) DK weight yarn, wool, in rust

Color F: 50yd/45m of (3) DK weight yarn, wool, in light green

Color G: 13yd/12m of (3) DK weight yarn, wool, in teal

Color H: 13yd/12m of (3) DK weight yarn, wool, in rose

Color I: 13yd/12m of (3) DK weight yarn, wool, in light purple

Color J: 13yd/12m of (3) DK weight yarn, wool, in lime

Color K: 13yd/12m of (3) DK weight yarn, wool, in spruce

Color L: 13yd/12m of (3) DK weight yarn, wool, in blue

Color M: 13yd/12m of (3) DK weight yarn, wool, in olive

Color N: 13yd/12m of (3) DK weight yarn, wool, in purple

Color O: 13yd/12m of (3) DK weight yarn, wool, in violet

Color P: 13yd/12m of (3) DK weight yarn, wool, in brown

Color Q: 13yd/12m of (3) DK weight yarn, wool, in red

Color R: 13yd/12m of (3) DK weight yarn, wool, in lilac

Color S: 13yd/12m of (3) DK weight yarn, wool, in gold

Color T: 13yd/12m of (3) DK weight yarn, wool, in pink

Color U: 13yd/12m of (3) DK weight yarn, wool, in salmon

Knitting needles: 3.25mm (size 3 U.S.) set of 4 double-pointed needles, *or size to obtain gauge*

Stitch marker

Yarn needle

GAUGE
28 sts and 24 rows = 4"/10cm in Fair Isle; 6-st rectangles = 1"/2.5cm wide x 1¼"/3cm long

Always take time to check your gauge.

CUFF
With A, cast on 48 sts. Distribute sts evenly over three needles (16 sts per needle). Place a stitch marker for beginning of round. Taking care not to twist sts, join to work in the round.

Round 1: Knit.

Round 2: Purl.

Round 3: Knit.

Round 4: Change to B, Knit.

6-st Foundation Triangles

Note: Triangles are worked back and forth in rows.

Row 1 (RS): K2, turn.

Row 2: Sl 1, p1.

Row 3: K3.

Row 4: Sl 1, p2.

Row 5: K4.

Row 6: Sl 1, p3.

Row 7: K5.

Row 8: Sl 1, p4.

Row 9: K6.

Repeat rows 1–9 around—8 triangles.

First Round of 6-st Rectangles

Row 1 (pick up row): With WS facing and C, beginning on any triangle, pick up and purl 5 sts down the side of the triangle, then purl a 6th st from the next triangle.

Row 2: K6.

Row 3: P5, p2tog.

Note: On these rows, you will purl together the last st of the previous row and the next st of the triangle on the left needle.

Repeat rows 2 and 3 until you have purled together all the sts of the next; end with a WS row. Repeat this process around all triangles—8 rectangles.

Second Round of 6-st Rectangles

With D, work in similar manner as for first round of 6-st rectangles. Pick up and purl sts up the side of each rectangle (rather than down the side of each foundation triangle)—8 rectangles. Push peaks to RS of work and pull out point with a needle.

Fill-in Triangles

Row 1 (pick up row): With RS facing and E, beginning on any rectangle; pick up and knit 5 sts along side of the rectangle, then knit a 6th st from the rectangle on the left needle.

Row 2: Sl 1, p1.

Row 3: Sl 1, k2.

Row 4: Sl 1, p3.

Row 5: Sl 1, k4.

Row 6: Sl 1, p5.

Row 7: Sl 1, k6.

Row 8: Sl 1, p5, p3tog.

Row 9: Sl 1, k5, sk2p.

Repeat rows 1–9 to fill in between all rectangles—8 triangles. Do not cut yarn.

Next round (RS): With RS facing, knit around, working k2tog between each triangle (8 sts decreased)—48 sts.

LEG

Next 3 rounds: *K1 with E, k1 with F; repeat from * around.

4-st Triangles

Work with F, repeat rows 1–5 of 6-st Foundation Triangles around—12 triangles.

First Round of 4-st Rectangles

Row 1 (pick up row): With WS facing and G, beginning on any triangle, pick up and purl 3 sts down the side of the triangle, then purl a 4th st from the next triangle.

Row 2: K4.

Row 3: P3, p2tog.

Repeat rows 2 and 3 until you have purled together all the sts of the next triangle; end with a WS row. Repeat this process around all triangles—12 rectangles.

Second Round of 4-st Rectangles

With H, work in similar manner as for first round of 4-st rectangles. Pick up and purl sts up the side of each rectangle (rather than down the side of each foundation triangle)—8 rectangles. Push peaks to RS of work and pull out point with a needle.

Third Round of 4-st Rectangles

Row 1 (pick up row): With RS facing and I, beginning on any rectangle, pick up and knit 3 sts down the side of the rectangle, then knit a 4th st from the next rectangle.

Row 2: P4.

Row 3: K3, ssk.

Repeat rows 2 and 3 until all the sts of the next rectangle have been consumed by the ssk; end with a RS row. Repeat this process around all rectangles—12 rectangles.

Fourth Round of 4-st Rectangles

With RS facing and J, work as for third round of 4-st rectangles.

Fill-in Triangles

Row 1 (pick-up row): With WS facing and K, pick up and purl 3 sts along side of rectangle, purl a 4th st from the next rectangle.

Row 2: Sl 1, k1.

Row 3: Sl 1, p2.

Row 4: Sl 1, k3.

Row 5: Sl 1, p4.

Row 6: Sl 1, k3, k2tog.

Row 7: Sl 1, p3 , p2tog.

Repeat rows 1–7 to fill in between all rectangles—12 triangles. Do not cut yarn.

Next round (RS): With RS facing, knit around, working k2tog between each triangle (12 sts decreased)—48 sts.

foot pattern chart

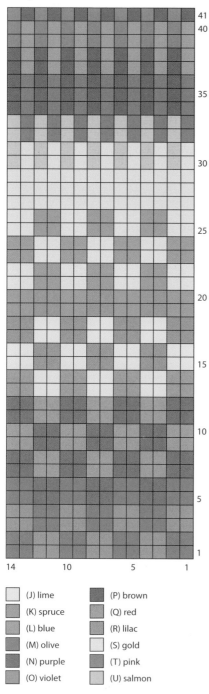

41
40
35
30
25
20
15
10
5
1

14   10   5   1

Color Key:
- (J) lime
- (K) spruce
- (L) blue
- (M) olive
- (N) purple
- (O) violet
- (P) brown
- (Q) red
- (R) lilac
- (S) gold
- (T) pink
- (U) salmon

The above are color suggestions only.
Use as many different colors as desired.

Ankle Stripes

Next 5 rounds: *K1 with K, k1 with L; repeat from * around.

Next 4 rounds: *K1 with M, k1 with L; repeat from * around.

Next 3 rounds: *K1 with M, k1 with N; repeat from * around.

Next 2 rounds: *K1 with M, k1 with O; repeat from * around. Cut all colors, except O.

HEEL FLAP

Redistribute stitches as follows. Place 24 sts on one needle (for heel flap), and 12 sts on each of two needles (for instep). The instep sts are held until after the heel flap has been knit and the heel turned. Work back and forth in rows over 24 heel sts only.

Row 1 (WS): (K1, p1) twice, p to last 4 sts, (k1, p1) twice.

Row 2 (RS): (P1, k1) twice, *sl 1 as if to purl, k1; repeat from * to last 4 sts, (p1, k1) twice.

Repeat these 2 rows for a total of 26 rows, then repeat last row once more.

Turn Heel

Row 1 (RS): K14, ssk, k1, turn.

Row 2: Sl 1, p5, p2tog, p1.

Row 3: Sl 1, k5, ssk, k1.

Row 4: Sl 1, p6, p2tog, p1.

Row 5: Sl 1, k7, ssk, k1.

Row 6: Sl 1, p8, p2tog, p1.

Row 7: Sl 1, k9, ssk, k1.

Row 8: Sl 1, p10, p2tog, p1.

Row 9: Sl 1, k11, ssk, k1.

Row 10: Sl 1, p12, p2tog.

Row 11: Knit—14 sts.

GUSSET

Pick-up round: With RS of heel facing and spare needle, knit the first 7 sts of the heel; with another needle knit remaining 7 heel sts, pick up and knit 14 sts along side of heel flap (needle #1); with two more needles knit across all sts of each instep needle (needles #2 and #3); with another needle pick up and k14 sts along opposite side of heel flap, then k7 sts from spare needle—66 sts (21 sts each on needles #1 and #4, 12 each on needles #2 and #3).

Round 1:

Needle #1: Knit to last 3 sts, ssk, k1—20 sts;

Needles #2 and #3: Knit to end;

Needle #4: Ssk, knit to end—20 sts (64 sts total).

Round 2: Knit across all sts on all four needles.

Repeat last 2 rounds four more times—56 sts remain (16 sts each on needles #1 and #4, 12 each on needles #2 and #3).

Slip 2 sts from needle #1 to needle #2, and 2 sts from needle #4 to needle #3—56 sts (14 sts on each needle).

FOOT

Continue is St st (knit every round) following Foot Pattern Chart. When length of foot reaches knuckle of big toe, stop working foot pattern. With C, work toe decreases as follows:

Shape Toe
Round 1:

Needle #1: Knit to last 3 sts, ssk, k1.

Needle #2: K2tog, knit to end.

Needle #3: Knit to last 3 sts, ssk, k1.

Needle #4: K2tog, knit to end.

Next round: Knit across all sts on all 4 needles.

Repeat last 2 rows until 6 sts remain on each needle; end with a knit round. Cut yarn, leaving a 12"/30.5cm tail.

Finish Toe
With WS facing, weave tail across sts on needle #1 so yarn is at side of sock. Distribute stitches onto two needles, one for the sole and the other for the top of the foot. Use Kitchener Stitch to sew the two sets of stitches together.

FINISHING
Weave in ends. Block if desired.

This project was knit with:

Kathryn Alexander Yarn's Hand-Dyed Wool, sport weight, 100% wool, approx 62yd/56m per skein. 1 skein each of 21 different colors was used. These are hand-dyed yarns prepared in small batches; there are no official color names.

knitty BITS

MY LOVE AFFAIR WITH SOCKS
BY KATHRYN ALEXANDER

I was planting trees for Scott Paper Company in the Pacific Northwest in the late '70s. We would drive to the planting site each morning in a big eight-man Suburban, aptly named "the crummy." Most days, in order to get out of the rain, the whole crew piled into the rig to eat lunch. The men on the crew played pinochle, as I happily read.

In my second year of planting trees, another woman was hired. She sat behind me during lunch and knit socks, which I thought would be a great use of my free time. And so during that season of planting trees, I learned to make socks, but tube socks were as far as I got. When planting season passed, I spent some time with my husband's great Aunt Hannah. She taught me how to turn a heel using directions handed out to Red Cross sock-knitters during WWII.

I could turn a heel now, but after leaving the security of the crummy and my knitting friend, who chose the yarn and needle size for me, gauge soon became the problem. I was filled with uncertainty. What seemed right in the swatch usually did not come true in the finished sock, resulting in many a sock that was so small I couldn't get it on over my arch or heel or so big that it would have fit over my boots.

I eventually met a knitting neighbor who was a great help. Now, I've moved on to a different issue—putting a project down. But that's one I can live with.

Kathryn Alexander is an internationally known textile artist—a spinner, weaver, dyer and knitter—whose work is characterized by an abundance of color, richly textured surfaces, and whimsical designs.

PREDICTABLE PATTERNS

BY LAURA BRYANT

A veritable cornucopia of delicious visual flavors awaits the adventurous knitter willing to explore hand-dyed yarns! We love all those yummy colors, and yet, very often, don't love the finished knitted product. Everyone who has tasted hand-dyed yarns has noticed the random pooling and patterning of colors that tend to happen when we least expect—or desire—it. What if you could tame that patterning and turn it to your own purposes? Well, you can with a few simple steps.

To determine the color repeat of hand-dyed yarn:

First, take a close look at the yarn. Identify a clean color break, where one color obviously becomes another. Follow along the strand until you find that color break again. With scrap yarn, chain 100 sts. With the suggested needle, beginning at the color break, pick up and knit through chain until the same color is reached again. This is a base-line number of stitches. Purl a row, and check to see that roughly the same place is reached at the end of the current row as in the prior row. The color break will be at the other end on the prior row. Natural variations in tension might require dropping or adding a few stitches. Knit another row, check again, and then purl one more row and recheck. At this point you should have settled into a tension and rhythm that allows all the colors to be used in one row. Our sample color, Autumn, contains four distinct colors: rust, olive, teal,

violet, and their overlaps. (Swatch A)

Work the base-line number of stitches back and forth in stockinette stitch, and an argyle-like pattern of diamonds will develop, as in Swatch B. The bottom portion, worked on a #3 needle with a gauge of 26 sts and 34 rows to 4 inches (10.2 cm), begins to pattern on 85 sts. You will see the central colors stacking up. At point 1, the needle size was changed to #2 for a gauge of 28 sts and 38 rows to 4 inches (10.2 cm). The colors run past the number of stitches and the patterning ceased, so stitches were increased to 94 by point 2, at which point patterning resumed. The long stretch of stockinette on this number of stitches shows how charming this type of patterning can be.

"But wait," you say, "socks are knit in the round." True enough, but the same numbers tell us what will happen when stockinette is worked in the round. The colors now will stack one upon another, as the number of stitches is calculated to use up the full run of colors in each round. Swatch C was worked on 94 stitches with #3 needles, and the colors can clearly be seen stacking, but the stockinette area is too large for socks. What causes knitting to pull in more than stockinette? Why, ribbing, of course. So the same number of stitches worked on the same size needle continues to stack colors, but pulls in much more. Is it the right size for socks? Well no, but with that number of stitches and gauge you could make great leg warmers!

swatch a

swatch b

point 2 | point 1

Well, what happens with fewer stitches? If you simply reduce the number of stitches, the patterning will be broken. Cut exactly in half, the yarn continues to pattern, but with a slight difference; the colors stack every other row instead of every row. Also, since hand-dyed yarns are not precise in their color stretches; the colors will move and combine in ever-changing variations. Swatches D and E show half the amount worked flat (43 stitches on # 3) and in the round (44 sts on # 3), respectively. E, smaller than an average sock, would be suitable for a child's sock or a small woman's sock. Too much fun!

Where else can this go? Well, if we want to base our sock on the full number of stitches, we must find stitches that use up more yarn per row so that we can have fewer stitches, giving us a smaller circumference. What might those be? Popcorns, twisted stitches, densely knitted traveling stitches—any of these are good candidates for using more yarn. We can also go the other way—find stitches that use up less yarn per row, like slipped stitches, which would allow us to go up from our half number for a larger circumference. With so many possibilities we'll leave the rest to your own inventiveness!

Laura Bryant is founder and owner of Prism Arts, Inc. A past president of The National Needlearts Association and current Vice President of Florida Craftsmen, she has published more than 36 pattern books for Prism Arts and has been featured in *American Craft* and *Fiberarts* magazines. Laura serves as a contributing editor for *Cast On* magazine—where she has a regular column called "The Art of Knitting"—and is on the Advisory Board for The Knitting Guild Association.

swatch c

swatch d

swatch e

137

Spring Fling

Ah, the sweetness of doing nothing, or as the Italians say, "il dolce far niente." There's nothing like kicking back on a sunny afternoon and watching the world go by.

SKILL LEVEL
Experienced

FINISHED MEASUREMENTS
Foot circumference: 7"/18cm

Leg length 5"/12.5cm

Foot length 8"/20.5cm

MATERIALS AND TOOLS
Approx total: 343yd/309m of (1) sock weight yarn, wool

Color A: 133yd/120m of (1) sock weight yarn, wool, in dark red

Color B: 210yd/189m of (1) sock weight yarn, wool, in medium pink

Knitting needles: 2.5mm (size 1½ U.S.) set of 4 double-pointed needles, and 2mm (size 0 U.S.) set of 4 double-pointed needles, *or size to obtain gauge*

Waste yarn

3 stitch markers

Stitch holder

Yarn needle

GAUGE
43 sts and 56 rows = 4"/10cm in Two-Color Cable Rib pattern using 2.5mm (size 1½ U.S.) needles

Always take time to check your gauge.

by KAREN NEAL

CUFF

Picot cast on: With smaller needles and A, cast on 3 sts using knitted cast-on method; *K2, bind off one stitch; slipping as if to purl, sl remaining st on right needle back on left needle (one small picot made); cast on 2 sts using knitted cast-on method; repeat from * until 35 sts are cast on.

Row 1: *K1, m1p (pick up the running strand between st on left needle and picot, using the left needle inserted from back to front, purl the new st through the front loop); repeat from * to last st, k1—69 sts.

Distribute stitches evenly over double-pointed needles. Taking care not to twist stitches, mark beginning and join to work in the round.

Round 1: P1, kfb, *k1, p1; repeat from * around—70 sts.

Rounds 2 and 3: *P1, k1; repeat from * around.

LEG

Change to larger needles.

Work in Two-Color Cable Rib pattern for 72 rounds (12 repeats) or until leg is desired length.

Note: Weave unused color strand up the inside of your work. At beginning of rounds, alternate carrying yarn B in front and then in back of yarn A, in order to carry the unused strand up the rows and weaving it in at the same time.

HEEL FLAP

Redistribute stitches as follows: Place first 35 sts on stitch holder (for instep); place last 35 sts on one needle (for heel flap).

With WS facing, working over 35 heel flaps sts only, and using B, sl 1 st wyif, p to end; DO NOT TURN.

With WS facing, using A, and working from beginning of row, work row 1 of Royal Quilting.

Note: Slipping the edge stitches at the beginning of rows as prescribed will create a lovely chain of stitches on the edges of your heel flap. Each of these slipped stitches will correspond to one gusset stitch to be picked up after the heel is turned.

Continue Royal Quilting for a total of 32 rows (4 repeats) or until heel flap is desired length from ankle bone to bottom of foot. End on row 8 or row 4.

Last Heel Flap Row (WS): With A, sl 1 wyif, p to last st, k1 tbl, turn.

Turn Heel

Row 1 (RS): With B, sl 1, k22, k2tog, k1, turn—9 sts unworked.

Row 2 (WS): With A, sl 1, p12, p2tog, p1, turn—9 sts unworked.

Row 3: With A, sl 1, k13, k2tog, k1, turn—7 sts unworked.

Row 4: With B, sl 1, p14, p2tog, p1, turn—7 sts unworked.

royal quilting

(multiples of 6 sts + 5; with slipped edges for heel flap)

Row 1 (WS: With A, sl 1 wyif, p2, *sl 5 wyib, p1, repeat from * to last 2 sts, p1, k1 tbl.

Row 2: Sl 1 color A st wyif, move strand of A to back between needles; with B, k to end.

Row 3: With B, sl 1 wyif, p to last st, k1 tbl.

Row 4: Sl 1 color B st wyif, move strand of B to back between needles; with A, k1, sl 3 wyib, *insert needle under the loose strand of row 1 and knit the next st, bringing st out under loose strand to catch strand behind st; sl 5 wyib; repeat from * to last 6 sts, knit next st under loose strand of row 1 (as before), sl 3 wyib, k2.

Row 5: With A, sl 1 wyif, p1, sl 3 wyib, *p1, sl 5 wyib; repeat from * to last 6 sts, p1, sl 3 wyib, p1, k1 tbl.

Rows 6 and 7: With B, repeat rows 2 and 3.

Row 8: Sl 1 color B st wyif, move B strand to back between needle; with A, k1, *knit next st under loose strand of row 5, sl 5 wyib; repeat from * to last 3 sts, knit next st under loose strand of row 5, k2.

Note: When working rows 1, 4, 5, and 8, carry long strand with loose but even tension across worked stitches.

two-color cable rib pattern

(multiples of 7 sts; worked in the round)

Round 1: With A, *p1, k6; repeat from * around.

Round 2: With A, *p1, sl 1 wyib, k4, sl 1 wyib; repeat from * around.

Rounds 3–5: With B, repeat round 2.

Round 6: With B, *p1, drop slipped st from left needle, k2, return dropped sl st to left needle and knit it, move next 2 sts from left needle to right needle, drop next slipped st from left needle, return 2 sts from right needle to left needle, return dropped sl st to left needle, k these 3 sts; repeat from * around.

Note: Dropping a slip stitch in round 6 feels a bit like jumping off a cliff...but dive on in! Since you have been slipping this stitch for the last 4 rows, it will be firmly cinched into your work and will remain facing you as you knit/redistribute the stitches. You will then be scooping it back onto your left needle and knitting it.

Repeat rows 1–6 for Two-Color Cable Rib pattern.

Row 5: With B, sl 1, k15, k2tog, k1, turn—5 sts unworked.

Row 6: With B, sl 1, p16, p2tog, p1, turn—5 sts unworked.

Row 7: With B, sl 1, k17, k2tog, k1, turn—3 sts unworked.

Row 8: With A, sl 1, p18, p2tog, p1, turn—3 sts unworked.

Row 9: With A, sl 1, k19, k2tog, k1, turn—1 st unworked.

Row 10: With B, sl 1, p20, p2tog, p1, turn—1 st unworked.

Row 11: With B, sl 1, k21, k2tog, turn—all sts worked.

Row 12: With B, sl 1, p21, p2tog, turn—all sts worked, with 23 sts live on heel (sole sts).

Row 13: With B, sl 1, k to end, do not turn.

Gusset Pick-Up

Slip held instep sts back onto a needle.

Round 1 (pick-up): With A, pick up and k18 sts along side of heel flap; corner gusset gap: On the heel flap side of work, lift a strand from the inside of the first stitch in the gap, place this strand on the instep needle and work it together, in pattern, with the first st of the instep; work remaining 34 instep sts in cable pattern as established; corner gusset gap: Lift a strand from the instep side of the gap and place on needle, in the next round work this st together with the first picked up st on this side of the heel flap; pick up and k18 sts along opposite side of heel flap; k across 23 sole sts.

Round 2 (pick-up): K18 tbl (gusset sts), AT THE SAME TIME, weave B strand behind these sts and leave it at the beginning of the instep sts; work 34 instep sts in cable pattern as established; k2tog tbl, k18 gusset sts tbl, k12 sole sts; mark new beginning of round—35 instep sts and 59 sole/gusset sts (94 sts total).

Note: Beginning of round is now at center of sole/heel stitches. Color strand changes occur at beginning of instep. Continue to work in established patterns; instep in Two-Color Cable Rib; sole and gusset in Stockinette St (k every round).

Shape Gusset
Note: Continue color striping pattern as established by instep Two-Color Cable Rib pattern.

Round 1: Knit to last 3 sts before instep sts, k2tog, k1; work 35 instep sts in cable pattern as established; k1, ssk, k to end.

Round 2: Work even in patterns as established, without decreasing.

Repeat rounds 1 and 2 until 62 sts remain on needles—35 instep sts and 27 sole sts.

Note: Fewer stitches are required for sole. There is a stitch gauge difference between the Stockinette Stitch sole (7¼ sts per inch/2.5cm) and the Cable Rib instep (10¾ sts per inch/2.5cm).

Continue in patterns as established without further decreases until foot measures 1½"/4cm less than desired length. End with Two-Color Cable Rib pattern row 6, or work with A in Stockinette Stitch to desired length.

Cut A, leaving a 6"/15cm tail.

Toe Set-Up Round: With B only, knit to 2 sts before instep sts, k2tog, k across instep sts, k2tog, k to end—60 sts.

Redistribute stitches evenly among needles and place markers after each set of 10 sts (or designate last stitch of needle as one of your "markers").

Shape Star Toe
Continue working with B only.

Round 1: *K to 2 sts before marker, k2tog; repeat from * to end—54 sts.

Round 2: Knit.

Repeat rounds 1 and 2 until 18 sts remain.

Next round: *K1, k2tog; repeat from * to end—12 sts.

Last decrease round: [K2tog] 6 times—6 sts.

Cut yarn leaving a 6"/15cm tail. Use yarn needle to weave tail through remaining sts, and pull tight.

FINISHING
Weave in ends.

This project was knit with:

Claudia's Hand Painted Yarns, fingering weight, 100% merino wool, 1.75oz/50g = approx 175yd/158m per skein (A) 1 skein, colorway "Crushed Velvet"
Koigu's KPM, fingering weight, 100% merino wool, 1.75oz/50g = approx 175yd/158m per skein (B) 2 skeins, #2233

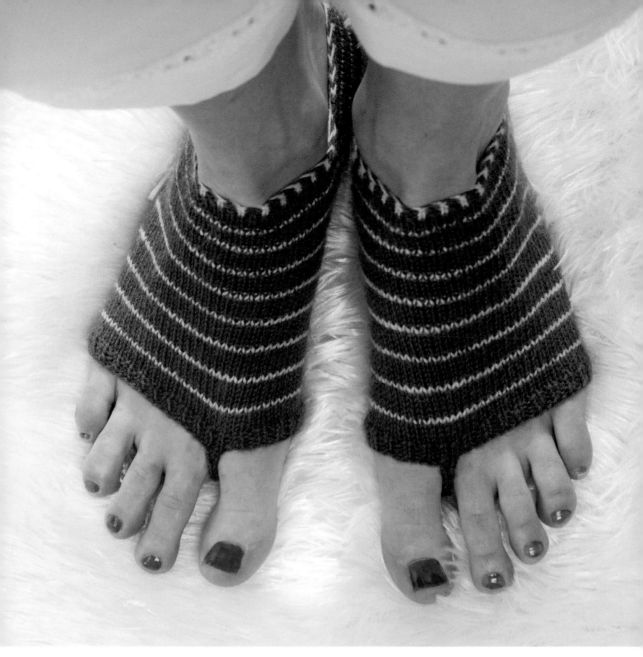

Peekaboo

Got plans to play a little footsy? Have your dainty digits look their best with a pedicure. Slip into these toeless ankle socks—complete with a sassy strap to hold them in place—for the ultimate spa treatment.

by KATE ATHERLEY

CUFF

Alternating A and B, cast on 56 (60, 64) sts onto one double-pointed needle. Ensure that the first stitch you work will be in B. Distribute the stitches evenly over three needles. Place a stitch marker for beginning of round. Taking care not to twist stitches, join to work in the round.

Round 1: *K1 with B, p1 with A; repeat from * around.

Repeat last round until cuff measures ½"/1.5cm from beginning.

HEEL FLAP

With A, work the first 28 (30, 32) sts of the next round (for heel flap). Place remaining 28 (30, 32) sts on a holder (for instep). Beginning with a WS row, and working back and forth on the 28 (30, 32) heel flap sts only, continue in Stockinette Stitch (k on RS, p on WS) as follows: Work 2 (2, 4) more rows with A, 1 row with B, 5 rows with A, 1 row with B, 5 rows with A, 1 row with B, 4 (6, 6) rows with A.

Turn Heel

Work with A only.

Foundation row (RS): K19 (20, 21), ssk, turn.

Row 1 (WS): Sl 1, p10, p2tog, turn.

Row 2 (RS): Sl 1, k10, ssk, turn.

Repeat rows 1 and 2 until all heel sts have been worked and 12 sts remain.

GUSSET

Pick-up round: With RS facing and A, k6 heel sts; with a new needle, k6 remaining heel sts, pick up and k14 (15, 16) sts along side of heel flap (needle #1); return the 28 (30, 32) instep sts from the holder to another needle and knit across them (needle #2); with another needle, pick up and k14 (15, 16) sts along the opposite side of the heel flap; with the same needle, k6 heel sts from the first needle (needle #3). The beginning of the round is now at the center of the heel.

Work in the following stripe pattern from here on: Work 5 rounds with A, 1 round with B. The pick-up round counts as the first round worked with A.

Next round: K6, k14 (15, 16) tbl (twisting picked-up sts), k28 (30, 32) instep sts, k14 (15, 16) tbl, k6.

57%

of sock knitters say they don't paint their toes— they're always wearing fabulous knitted socks.

SOCKTALK KATE ATHERLEY on....sock traditions

"It's always felt pretty natural to me, sock knitting. There's a story in my family that my grandmother used to earn money by charging her neighbors a penny to turn the heel of socks they were knitting."

Decrease round:

Needle #1: Knit to last 3 sts, k2tog, k1.

Needle #2: Knit.

Needle #3: K1, ssk, knit to end.

Next round: Knit.

Repeat the last 2 rounds until needles #1 and #3 each have 14 (15, 16) sts—56 (60, 64) sts.

Continue even in stripe pattern until foot measures 6 (6¼, 6¾)"/15 (16, 17)cm measured from back of heel. Cut B.

Next 3 rounds (K1, p1 Rib): With A, *k1, p1; repeat from * around.

Form Toe Thong

Right Sock Only: Working in K1, p1 Rib pattern, bind off 32 (34, 36) sts, work 3 sts and sl these 3 sts to a safety pin or stitch holder, bind off remaining sts.

Left Sock Only: Working in K1, p1 Rib pattern, bind off 22 (24, 26) sts, work 3 sts and sl these 3 sts to a safety pin or stitch holder, bind off remaining sts.

Both Socks: Rejoin A to 3 held sts, work 1½"/4cm in K1, p1 Rib pattern. Bind off. Sew the end of the thong to the underside of the sock opening lined up so that it sits between the big and second toes.

FINISHING
Weave in ends.

This project was knit with:

Sandnes Yarn's Sisu, fingering weight, 80% virgin wool, 20% nylon (polyamide), 1.75oz/50g = approx 174yd/157m per ball
(A) 1 ball, #4517 bright pink
(B) 1 ball, #8514 lime

Snow Bunny

Moguls and black diamond trails don't stand a chance against curve-hugging knee-highs.

by ANN KINGSTONE

SKILL LEVEL
Experienced

FINISHED MEASUREMENTS
Foot circumference 9¾"/25cm

Calf circumference (at widest)
  14"/35.5cm

Foot length 9½"/24cm

Leg length 14½"/37cm

MATERIALS AND TOOLS
Approx total: 880yd/792m of  fingering weight yarn, wool/nylon blend

  Color A: 440yd/396m of fingering weight yarn, wool/nylon, in pink

  Color B: 440yd/396m of fingering weight yarn, wool/nylon, in black

Knitting needles: 2.5mm (size 1½ U.S.) set of 5 double-pointed needles, *or size to obtain gauge*

Approx 40yd/36m knitting-in elastic

2 stitch holders or waste yarn

Yarn needle

GAUGE
32 sts and 44 rows = 4"/10cm in stranded pattern

Always take time to check your gauge.

CUFF

With A, cast on 104 sts (or more, in increments of 4 sts for each ½"/1.5cm of girth greater than 14"/35.5cm). Distribute the stitches evenly over four needles (26 sts per needle). Place a stitch marker for beginning of round. Taking care not to twist stitches, join to work in the round.

Holding one strand each of B and knitting-in elastic together, join B and elastic.

Next 10 rounds: *With A, k2; with B and elastic, p2; repeat from * around.

LEG

Follow the leg chart. Each round contains two repeats of the leg chart. If knitting for greater girth, take note of the four insertion points for extra stitches in each round (marked in red above the relevant column).

 Note: The decreases shown in black are worked for all sizes. The decreases shown in white are worked if knitting for greater girth only.

After round 125, follow the leg chart for the first half of each round, and then the heel setup chart for the latter half of each round.

After round 131, knit the next 4 sts with B and turn—78 sts.

HEEL FLAP

Row 1 (WS): With one needle, p39 in pattern shown in first row of heel chart. Place the remaining 39 sts onto waste yarn or stitch holder (for instep). Working back and forth on heel sts only, continue working heel chart, until chart is complete.

Turn Heel

The stranded pattern on the sole of the foot (the same pattern as on heel) is set up as the heel is turned. When decreasing stitches at either side, knit the decrease and the stitch that follows it in the appropriate color to continue the stranded pattern as it is worked in the current row, not according to the way those stitches were worked in the pattern in the preceding rows. Working the stranded pattern in this manner, proceed as follows:

Row 1 (RS): Sl 1, k21, ssk, k1.

Row 2 (WS): Sl 1, p6, p2tog, p1, turn.

Row 3: Sl 1, k to 1 st before the gap, ssk, k1, turn.

Row 4: Sl 1, p to 1 st before the gap, p2tog, p1, turn.

Repeat rows 3 and 4 until all heel sts have been worked and 23 sts remain.

INSTEP AND GUSSET

Redistribute stitches as follows: With RS of heel facing and continuing the stranded pattern, knit the first 12 sts of the heel onto a spare needle and hold away from work; with another needle, k the remaining 11 heel sts; with same needle, extending the stranded pattern into the gusset sts and knitting the last 2 sts with B, pick up and k16 along side of heel flap (needle #1); with another needle, work first 20 sts of first row of instep chart (needle #2); with another needle, work last 19 sts of first row of instep chart (needle #3); with another needle, extending the stranded pattern back over these sts (count back from the heel sts to calculate the placement of the stranded pattern), and knitting the first 2 sts with B, pick up and k16 sts along opposite side of heel flap, knit the heel sts from the spare needle (needle #4). You should now have 27 sts on needle #1, 20 sts on needle #2, 19 sts on needle #3, and 28 sts on needle #4.

Round 1:

Needle #1: Knit in stranded pattern as established to last 2 sts; with B, k2.

Needles #2 and #3: Continue working instep chart.

Needle #4: With B, k2; k remaining sts in stranded pattern as established.

Round 2:

Needle #1: Knit in stranded pattern as established to last 3 sts; with B, k2tog, k1.

Needles #2 and #3: Continue working instep chart.

Needle #4: With B, k1, ssk; k remaining sts in stranded pattern as established.

Repeat rounds 1 and 2 until needle #1 has 19 sts and needle #4 has 20 sts (78 sts total).

Work rounds in patterns as established, without further decreasing, through round 41 of instep chart. End ready to work stitches on needle #2.

Note: If knitting the longer foot size, change to the toe extension chart after round 38 and continue through round 49 of extension chart.

SHAPE TOE

Continue to work in patterns as established, following toe chart, and working decrease rounds as follows:

Decrease Round:

Needle #2: Continue working instep chart, working decrease as ssk.

Needle #3: Continue working instep chart, working decrease as k2tog.

Needle #4: With B, k1, ssk; knit to end in stranded pattern as established.

Needle #1: Knit to last 3 sts in stranded pattern as established; with B, k2tog, k1.

After the last round has been worked, cut the yarn leaving a 12"/30.5cm tail. Thread tail onto a yarn needle and thread it through the remaining sts, removing them from the needles. Draw the thread tight to close the toe.

FINISHING

Weave in ends. Block on sock blockers or with an iron under a damp cloth.

This project was knit with:

Lang Jawoll's Sock Yarn including reinforcement yarn, sock weight, 75% superwash new wool/18% nylon/7% acrylic, approx 1.5oz/45g = 220yd/198m per ball
(A) 2 balls, #772 pink
(B) 2 balls, #0004 black

leg (part 1)

leg (part 2)

 (A) pink

(B) black

/ k2tog

\ ssk

/ k2tog (larger sizes only)

\ ssk (larger sizes only)

instep and toe chart

heel chart

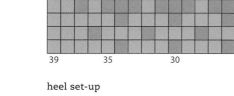

5

repeat
5 times
(total)

1

39   35   30   25   20   15   10   5   1

heel set-up

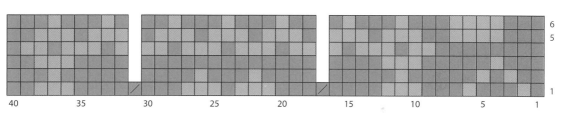

6
5

1

40   35   30   25   20   15   10   5   1

toe extension

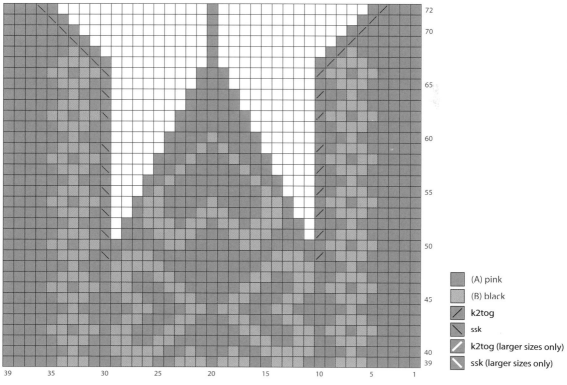

72
70
65
60
55
50
45
40
39

39   35   30   25   20   15   10   5   1

■ (A) pink
■ (B) black
◪ k2tog
◪ ssk
◪ k2tog (larger sizes only)
◪ ssk (larger sizes only)

Sole Mates

While he's embracing you, let these ribbed lovelies hug your feet. Soft, subtle, and with a killer diamond design up the back, these socks will have you feeling fresh and clean.

SKILL LEVEL
Experienced

FINISHED MEASUREMENTS
Foot circumference 9"/23cm

Leg length 8½"/21.5cm

Foot length 8½"/21.5cm

MATERIALS AND TOOLS
Approx total: 375yd/338m of
(1) fingering weight yarn,
wool/bamboo/nylon blend,
in misty blue variegated

Knitting needles: 2.75mm
(size 2 U.S.) set of 5
double-pointed needles,
or size to obtain gauge

Cable needle

Stitch markers (optional)

Yarn needle

GAUGE
30 sts and 40 rows = 4"/10cm
in Stockinette Stitch (knit
every round)

*Always take time to check
your gauge.*

by ALYSON JOHNSON

CUFF

Cast on 70 sts onto one needle. Distribute the stitches over four needles as follows: 17 sts each on needles #1 and #3, 18 sts each on needles #2 and #4. Place a stitch marker for beginning of round. Taking care not to twist stitches, join to work in the round.

Work in K1, p1 Ribbing until piece measures 1"/2.5cm from beginning.

LEG

Round 1:

Needle #1: Work row 1 of Seeded Cable chart (for back of leg);

Needles #2, #3, and #4: Work in Seeded Rib pattern (for remainder of leg).

Continue in patterns as established; working Seeded Cable chart over sts of needle #1, and Seeded Rib pattern over sts of needles #2, #3, and #4; work Seeded Cable chart twice or desired number of whole repeats. End with round 36 of chart.

Note: On the final round of the leg, stop working the Seeded Rib pattern 9 stitches before the end of the round (on needle #4). The heel flap will begin here.

CABLED HEEL FLAP

Note: The Seeded Cable pattern is located down the middle of the back of the leg.

Redistribute stitches as follows: Onto one needle, slip the last 9 sts of needle #4, the 17 sts of needle #1, and the first 9 sts of needle #2—35

sts. The remaining 35 stitches are held (for instep). Work back and forth on these heel stitches only.

Row 1 (RS): Sl 1, p14, k5, p15.

Row 2: Sl 1, k14, p5, k15.

Row 3: Sl 1, p14, C5FP, p15.

Row 4: Sl 1, k14, p5, k15.

Row 5: Sl 1, p14, k5, p15.

Row 6: Sl 1, k14, p5, k15.

Repeat these 6 rows three more times (24 rows total).

Turn Heel

Row 1 (RS): Sl 1, k19, k3tog, k1, turn (notice the double decrease, it appears in this row only).

Row 2: Sl 1, p7, p2tog, p1, turn.

Row 3: Sl 1, knit to one stitch before gap, k2tog over gap, k1, turn.

Row 4: Sl 1, purl to one stitch before gap, p2tog over gap, p1, turn.

Continue working in this manner, decreasing over the gap, until all stitches have been worked and 20 sts remain.

Note: On the last two rows, there will be no extra stitch to work after the decrease.

Pick-up round: With RS of heel facing and a spare needle, knit across first 10 heel sts; with another needle, knit across next 10 heel sts, pick up and knit 13 sts along side of heel flap (needle #1); with another needle, work in established Seeded Rib pattern across first 17 instep sts (needle #2); with another needle, continue in established Seeded Rib pattern across remaining instep

seeded rib pattern

· · · · · · · · · · · · · · · · · · ·

Round 1: Purl.

Round 2: *P2, k1; repeat from * to last 2 sts, p2.

Repeat rounds 1 and 2 for Seeded Rib pattern.

seeded cable

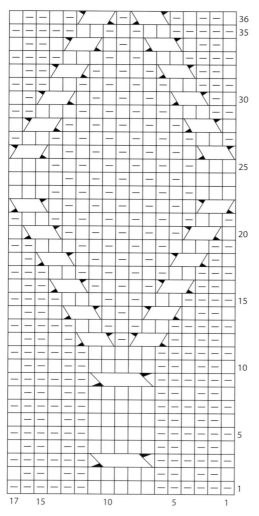

17   15   10   5   1

⬜ k on RS, p on WS

⊟ p on RS, k on WS

▱ C3Fp: Cable 3 Front purl - sl 2 sts onto cn and hold in front, p1, k2 from cn

▱ C3Bp: Cable 3 Back purl - sl 1 st onto cn and hold in back, k2, p1 from cn

▱ C5Fp: Cable 5 Front purl - sl 3 sts onto cn and hold in front, k2, (p1, k2) from cn

sts (needle #3); with another needle, pick up and knit 13 sts along opposite side of heel flap, knit 10 heel sts from spare needle (needle #4). You should now have 23 sts each on needles #1 and #4 (for gusset); 17 sts on needle #2, and 18 sts on needle #3 (for instep)—81 sts.

Shape Gusset
Round 1:

  Needle #1: Knit;

  Needles #2 and #3: Continue in Seeded Rib pattern as established;

  Needle #4: Knit.

Round 2:

  Needle #1: Knit to last 3 sts, k2tog, k1—22 sts;

  Needles #2 and #3: Continue in Seeded Rib pattern as established—35 sts;

  Needle #4: K1, ssk, knit to end—22 sts (79 sts total).

Repeat last 2 rounds until there are 17 sts each on needles #1 and #4—69 sts.

Work rounds in established pattern, without further de-creasing, until foot measures 6½"/16.5cm, or 2½"/6.5cm less than desired total foot length; end ready to work stitches from needle #1 (center back/sole).

Shape Toe
Round 1:

  Needle #1: Knit to last 3 sts, k2tog, k1—16 sts;

  Needle #2: P1, ssp, purl to end—16 sts;

Needle #3: Purl to last 4 sts, p3tog, p1—16 sts (notice double decrease);

Needle #4: K1, ssk, knit to end—16 sts (64 sts total).

Round 2:

Needles #1 and #4: Knit.

Needles #2 and #3: Purl.

Round 3:

Needle #1: Knit to last 3 sts, k2tog, k1—15 sts;

Needle #2: P1, ssp, purl to end—15 sts;

Needle #3: Purl to last 3 sts, p2tog, p1—15 sts;

Needle #4: K1, ssk, knit to end—15 sts.

Round 4: Repeat round 2.

Repeat the last 2 rounds until 5 sts remain on each needle.

Finish Toe

Next round: Knit sts of needle #1 onto needle #4; slip sts of needle #2 onto needle #3, so there are now two needles with 10 sts on each. Cut yarn, leaving a 14"/35.5cm tail. Use Kitchener Stitch to sew the two sets of stitches together.

FINISHING
Weave in ends.

This project was knit with:

Zen Yarn Garden's Bamboolicious, fingering weight, 70% superwash merino, 20% bamboo, 10% nylon, 4oz/113g = approx 450yd/405m per skein 1 skein, tranquility

SOCKTALK ALYSON JOHNSON on... being a socks-aholic

"You're either into socks, or you're not. Sock people don't really 'get' non-socks-people, and vice versa—but we do our best to try to convert everyone we can!"

Golden Dahlia

Your life may be lacking in dashing investigators, but your socks should still be intriguing. This regal pair should do the trick, featuring a fancy lace panel with twisted stitches in the front and back, and simple twisted cables up the sides.

by KIRSTEN KAPUR

SKILL LEVEL
Experienced

FINISHED MEASUREMENTS
Foot circumference 7½"/19cm

Leg length 8½"/21.5cm

Foot length custom

MATERIALS AND TOOLS
Approx total: 350yd/315m of (1) fingering weight yarn, wool, in gold

Knitting needles: 2.25mm (size 1 U.S.) 2 circular needles 24"/61cm long, and 2.25mm (size 1 U.S.) 1 double-pointed needle, *or size to obtain gauge*

Stitch marker

Cable needle

Yarn needle

GAUGE
34 sts and 42 rows = 4"/10cm in Dahlia Stitch pattern (see chart)

Always take time to check your gauge.

twisted rib (over an even number of sts)

Round 1: *K1 tbl, p1; repeat from * around.
Repeat round 1 for Twisted Rib pattern.

CUFF

Cast on 64 sts onto one circular needle. Transfer 32 stitches to second needle. Place a stitch marker for beginning of round. Taking care not to twist stitches, join to work in the round.

Work in Twisted Rib pattern for 10 rounds.

LEG

Work Dahlia Leg pattern (see Dahlia Leg chart) for 59 total rounds.

HEEL FLAP

Transfer last stitch of needle #1 onto needle #2. There are now 31 stitches on needle #1 (for heel) and 33 stitches on needle #2 (for instep). Work back and forth on heel stitches only.

Row 1 (RS): Sl 1, *(k1 tbl, p1); repeat from * across.

Row 2 (WS): Sl 1, *(p1 tbl, k1); repeat from * across.

Repeat last 2 rows eleven more times (24 rows total) or until heel flap measures 2¼"/6cm.

Turn Heel

Continue to work back and forth on heel stitches only.

Row 1 (RS): Sl 1, k17, k2tog, k1, turn.

Row 2 (WS): Sl 1, p6, p2tog, p1, turn.

Row 3: Sl 1, k7, k2tog, k1, turn.

Continue working in this manner, working one additional stitch before the decrease on each row, until 19 stitches remain, ending with a RS row.

Note: On the last row, there will be no extra stitch to work after the decrease.

GUSSET

Pick-up round: With RS of heel facing and needle #1, pick up and knit 13 stitches along side of heel flap; with needle #2, work row 1 of Dahlia Foot pattern over instep stitches (see Dahlia Foot chart); with the double-pointed needle, pick up and knit 13 stitches along opposite side of heel flap,

knit across stitches of needle #1, slip all these stitches onto needle #1; with needle #2, work row 2 of Dahlia Foot pattern over instep stitches—78 sts (45 sts on needle #1, and 33 sts on needle #2).

Round 1:

Needle #1: K1, ssk, knit to last 3 sts, k2tog, k1;

Needle #2: Continue in established foot pattern.

Round 2:

Needle #1: Knit;

Needle #2: Continue in established foot pattern.

Repeat last 2 rounds until 31 stitches remain on needle #1—64 sts.

FOOT

Continue to knit across needle #1 and work from Dahlia Foot chart across needle #2 until foot measures 1½"/4cm less than desired length.

Shape Toe

Transfer first stitch of needle #2 back onto needle #1. There are now 32 sts on each needle.

Round 1:

Needle #1: K1, ssk, knit to last 3 sts, k1, k2tog, k1;

Needle #2: Work as for needle #1.

Round 2: Knit.

Repeat last two rounds until 12 stitches remain on each needle.

Repeat round 1 only until 8 stitches remain on each needle.

off the charts

dahlia foot chart

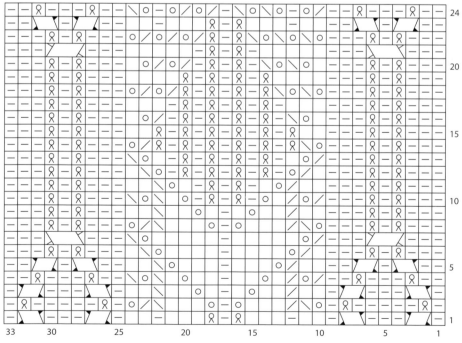

Finish Toe

Cut yarn, leaving an 8"/20.5cm tail. Use Kitchener Stitch to sew the two sets of stitches together.

FINISHING

Weave in ends.

This project was knit with:

Koigu's Premium Merino, sock weight, 100% merino wool, 1.75oz/50g = approx 175yd/158m per skein 2 skeins, #2100

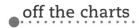

off the charts

dahlia leg chart

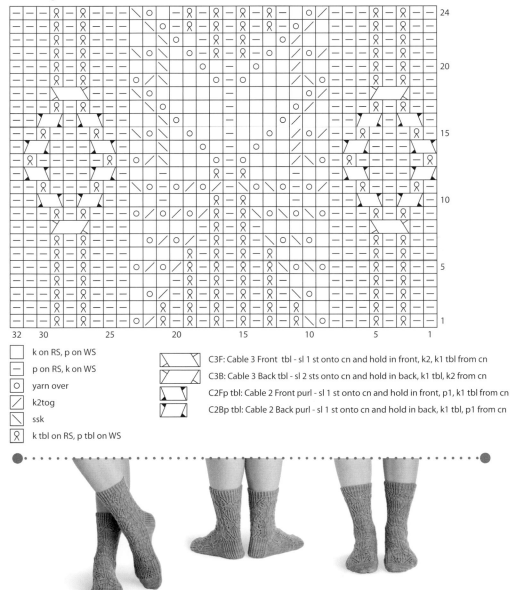

	k on RS, p on WS
−	p on RS, k on WS
o	yarn over
/	k2tog
\	ssk
Ⴖ	k tbl on RS, p tbl on WS

C3F: Cable 3 Front tbl - sl 1 st onto cn and hold in front, k2, k1 tbl from cn

C3B: Cable 3 Back tbl - sl 2 sts onto cn and hold in back, k1 tbl, k2 from cn

C2Fp tbl: Cable 2 Front purl - sl 1 st onto cn and hold in front, p1, k1 tbl from cn

C2Bp tbl: Cable 2 Back purl - sl 1 st onto cn and hold in back, k1 tbl, p1 from cn

Sweet Nothings

Lacy and daintily beaded, there's something alluring about so much knitted innocence.

by PAULINE SCHULTZ

CUFF

Cast on 84 (96, 108) sts onto one needle. Distribute the stitches evenly over three needles (28 (32, 36) sts per needle). Place a stitch marker for beginning of round. Taking care not to twist stitches, join to work in the round.

Ankle Ribbing

Work Cuff Ruffle Pattern.

Work Cuff Honeycomb Pattern.

Next 4 (5, 5) rounds: Knit.

Next round (picot edge for cuff fold-over): *Yo, k2tog; repeat from * around.

Next 3 (4, 4) rounds: Knit.

Next round: Knit, increasing 2 (4, 6) sts evenly—30 (36, 42) sts.

Turn work inside out. To minimize the hole caused by working back on the same row, purl together the first st on needle #1 and the purl bump from the last st on needle #3. Work in P1, K1 Rib for 2 (2, 3)"/5 (5, 7.5)cm.

Ankle Lace

Rounds 1, 3, 5, and 7: Knit.

Round 2: *Yo, ssk, k1, k2tog, yo, k1; repeat from * around.

Round 4: *Yo, k1, sk2p, k1, yo, k1; repeat from * around.

Round 6: *K2tog, yo, k1, yo, ssk, k1; repeat from * around.

Round 8: K1 and slip to needle #3, *(k1, yo) twice, k1, sk2p; repeat from * around.

Rounds 9–16 (24, 32): Repeat last 8 rounds 1 (2, 3) more times.

SKILL LEVEL
Intermediate

FINISHED MEASUREMENTS
Foot circumference 5½ (7, 7½)"/14 (18, 19)cm

Leg length 7½ (8½, 10½)"/19 (21.5, 26.5)cm

Foot length 8½ (9½, 10)"/21.5 (24, 25.5)cm

MATERIALS AND TOOLS
Approx total: 274 (274, 411) yd/247 (247, 370)m of **③** DK weight yarn, wool/cashmere/microfiber, in off white

Knitting needles: 3.75mm (size 5 U.S.) set of 4 double-pointed needles, *or size to obtain gauge*

16 pearl beads—6mm diameter

Stitch marker

Yarn needle

GAUGE
24 sts and 30 rows = 4"/10cm in Stockinette Stitch (knit every round)

24 sts and 34 rows = 4"/10cm in Lace Pattern

Always take time to check your gauge.

foot lace pattern

Rounds 1, 3, 5, and 7: Knit.

Size Small only:

Round 2: K1, (yo, ssk, k1, k2tog, yo, k1) 3 times, yo, ssk, k1.
Round 4: K1, (yo, k1, sk2p, k1, yo, k1) 3 times, yo, k1, ssk.
Round 6: K1, (k2tog, yo, k1, yo, ssk, k1) 3 times, k2tog, yo, k1.
Round 8: Ssk, (k1, yo) twice, k1, [sk2p, (k1, yo) twice, k1] twice, sk2p, k1, yo, k1.

Size Medium only:

Round 2: K1, (k2tog, yo, k1, yo, ssk, k1) 4 times.
Round 4: Ssk, [(k1, yo) twice, k1, sk2p] 3 times, (k1, yo) twice, k1, ssk.
Round 6: K1, (yo, ssk, k1, k2tog, yo, k1) 4 times.
Round 8: K1, (yo, k1, sk2p, k1, yo, k1) 4 times.

Size Large only:

Round 2: K1, (yo, ssk, k1, k2tog, yo, k1) 4 times, yo, ssk, k1.
Round 4: K1, (yo, k1, sk2p, k1, yo, k1) 4 times, yo, k1, ssk.
Round 6: K1, (k2tog, yo, k1, yo, ssk, k1) 4 times, k2tog, yo, k1.
Round 8: Ssk, [(k1, yo) twice, k1, sk2p] 4 times, k1, yo, k1.
Repeat rounds 1–8 for Foot Lace Pattern.

cuff ruffle pattern (Bell Pattern)

Round 1 and 2: *P3, k9; repeat from * around.
Round 3: *P3, ssk, k5, k2tog; repeat from * around—70 (80, 90) sts.
Round 4: *P3, k7; repeat from * around.
Round 5: *P3, ssk, k3, k2tog; repeat from * around—56 (64, 72) sts.
Round 6: *P3, k5; repeat from * around.
Round 7: *P3, ssk, k1, k2tog; repeat from * around—42 (48, 54) sts.
Round 8: *P3, k3; repeat from * around.
Round 9: *P3, sk2p; repeat from * around—28 (32, 36) sts.
Round 10: *P3, k1; repeat from * around.

cuff honeycomb pattern

Rounds 1–5: Purl.
Round 6: *P3, drop next st off needle and unravel down 5 rows, purl together unraveled st and the 5 unraveled strands; repeat from * around.
Rounds 7–11: Purl.
Round 12: *P1, drop next st off needle and unravel down 5 rows, purl together unraveled st and the 5 unraveled strands, p2; repeat from * around.
Rounds 13–18: Repeat rounds 1–6.

Create Back Heel

K2, slip these sts to previous needle, m1, k10 (13, 16), m1, knit to end of round.

Work back and forth on the first 12 (15, 18) sts on needle #1, as follows:

Rows 1, 3, 5, and 7: Purl.

Size Small only:

Row 2: K2, k2tog, yo, k1, yo, ssk, k1, k2tog, yo, k2.

Row 4: K1, ssk, (k1, yo) twice, k1, sk2p, k1, yo, k2.

Row 6: K2, yo, ssk, k1, k2tog, yo, k1, yo, ssk, k2.

Row 8: K2, yo, k1, sk2p, (k1, yo) twice, k1, ssk, k1.

Size Medium only:

Row 2: K2, (k2tog, yo, k1, yo, ssk, k1) twice, k1.

Row 4: K1, ssk, (k1, yo) twice, k1, sk2p, (k1, yo) twice, k1, ssk, k1.

Row 6: K2, (yo, ssk, k1, k2tog, yo, k1) twice, k1.

Row 8: K2, (yo, k1, sk2p, k1, yo, k1) twice, k1.

Size Large only:

Row 2: K2, (k2tog, yo, k1, yo, ssk, k1) twice, k2tog, yo, k2.

Row 4: K1, ssk, [(k1, yo) twice, k1, sk2p] twice, k1, yo, k2.

Row 6: K2, (yo, ssk, k1, k2tog, yo, k1) twice, yo, ssk, k2.

Row 8: K2, (yo, k1, sk2p, k1, yo, k1) twice, yo, k1, ssk, k1.

All Sizes:

Rows 9–20 (28, 32): Repeat last 8 rows 1 (2, 3) more time(s); then repeat rows 1–4, 1 (1, 0) more time(s).

Row 21 (29, 33): Purl, increasing 0 (1, 0) st at midpoint—12 (16, 18) sts.

Turn Heel

Row 1: K7 (9, 9), ssk, k1, turn.

Row 2: Sl 1, p3, p2tog, p1, turn.

Row 3: Sl 1, k4, ssk, k1, turn.

Continue as established in rows 2 and 3, knitting or purling one more stitch than the previous row, until all stitches are consumed—8 (10, 11) sts remain.

Size Large only:

Next row: Purl, increasing 1 st at the midpoint—8 (10, 12) sts.

All Sizes:

Rearrange stitches so that half the heel stitches are on needle #1—4 (5, 6) sts, all instep stitches are on needle #2—20 (23, 26) sts, and the remaining heel stitches are on needle #3 (center back and end of round)—4 (5, 6) sts. Knit the stitches on needle #3.

Shape Gusset
Round 1:

Needle #1: Knit the heel stitches on needle #1, then pick up and knit 9 (11, 13) stitches up the side of the heel—13 (16, 19) sts.

Needle #2: With free needle, work across the instep stitches, as follows:

Size Small only: M1, (yo, ssk, k1, k2tog, yo, k1) 3 times, yo, ssk, m1—22 sts.

Size Medium only: M1, (k2tog, yo, k1, yo, ssk, k1) 3 times, ssk, yo, k1, yo, k2tog, m1—25 sts.

Size Large only: M1, (yo, ssk, k1, k2tog, yo, k1) 4 times, yo, ssk, m1—28 sts.

Needle #3: Pick up and knit 9 (11, 13) sts down side heel, knit heel stitches on needle #3—13 (16, 19) sts.

Round 2:

Needle #1: Knit to last 3 sts, k2tog, k1—12 (15, 18) sts;

Needle #2: Knit—22 (25, 28) sts;

Needle #3: K1, ssk, k to end—12 (15, 18) sts.

Round 3:

Needle #1: Knit;

Needle #2: Beginning with round 4 of appropriate size, work Foot Lace Pattern;

Needle #3: Knit—46 (55, 64) sts.

Repeat last 2 rounds 6 (7, 9) more times—34 (41, 46) sts remain.

Work rounds in established pattern, without further decreasing until sock measures 7½ (8½, 9)"/19 (21.5, 23)cm from heel back, ending with row 8 of Foot Lace Pattern.

Shape Toe
Size Small only:

Round 1: K6, k2tog, k18, ssk, k6—32 sts.

Round 2: K6, k2tog, (k1, k2tog, yo, k1, yo, ssk) twice, k1, k2tog, yo, k1, ssk, k6—30 sts.

Round 3: K6, k2tog, k14, ssk, k6—28 sts.

Round 4: K6, k2tog, k2, yo, k1, sk2p, (k1, yo) twice, k1, ssk, k1, ssk, k6—26 sts.

Round 5: K6, k2tog, k10, ssk, k6—24 sts.

Round 6: K6, k2tog, (k1, yo) twice, ssk, k1, k2tog, k1, ssk, k6—22 sts.

Round 7: K4, ssk, k2tog, k6, ssk, k2tog, k4—18 sts.

Round 8: K3, ssk, k2tog, (yo, k1) twice, ssk, k2, k2tog, k3—16 sts.

Size Medium only:

Round 1: K8, k2tog, k21, ssk, k8—39 sts.

Round 2: K8, k2tog, (k1, yo, ssk, k1, k2tog, yo) 3 times, k1, ssk, k8—37 sts.

Round 3: K8, k2tog, k17, ssk, k8—35 sts.

Round 4: K10, [sk2p, (k1, yo) twice, k1] twice, sk2p, k10—33 sts.

Round 5: K6, ssk, k2tog, k13, ssk, k2tog, k6—29 sts.

Round 6: K5, ssk, k2tog, yo, k2tog, k1, ssk, yo, k1, yo, k2tog, k1, ssk, yo, ssk, k2tog, k5—25 sts.

Round 7: K4, ssk, k2tog, k9, ssk, k2tog, k4—21 sts.

Round 8: K3, ssk, (k2tog) twice, (k1, yo) twice, k1, (ssk) twice, k2tog, k3—17 sts.

Size Large only:

Round 1: K9, k2tog, k24, ssk, k9—44 sts.

Round 2: K9, k2tog, (k1, k2tog, yo, k1, yo, ssk) 3 times, k1, k2tog, yo, k1, ssk, k9—42 sts.

Round 3: K9, k2tog, k20, ssk, k9—40 sts.

Round 4: K9, k2tog, k1, (k1, yo, k1, sk2p, k1, yo) twice, k1, yo, k1, ssk, k1, ssk, k9—38 sts.

Round 5: K9, k2tog, k16, ssk, k9—36 sts.

Round 6: K7, ssk, (k2tog) twice, (yo, k1, yo, ssk, k1, k2tog) twice, yo, ssk, k2tog, k7—32 sts.

Round 7: K6, ssk, k2tog, k12, ssk, k2tog, k6—28 sts.

Round 8: K5, ssk, k2tog, k1, yo, k1, sk2p, (k1, yo) twice, k1, (ssk) twice, k2tog, k5—24 sts.

Finish Toe

Knit 4 (4, 6) stitches. Slip these stitches to previous needle (needle #1 to needle #3). Turn sock inside out, and join toe stitches using 3-needle bind off.

FINISHING

Weave in ends. Sew one pearl into center of each Honeycomb box of Ankle.

This project was knit with:

Debbie Bliss's Baby Cashmerino, DK weight, 55% Merino wool/33% cashmere/12% microfiber, 1.75oz/50g = approx 137yd/123m per ball 2 (2, 3) balls, #340100 off white

bell pattern

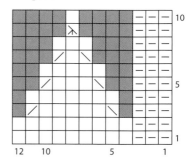

honeycomb pattern

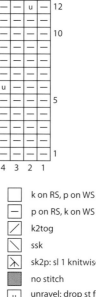

	k on RS, p on WS
—	p on RS, k on WS
/	k2tog
\	ssk
⋏	sk2p: sl 1 knitwise, k2tog, psso
▨	no stitch
u	unravel: drop st from needle and unraveldown 5 rows; purl together the unravelled st with the 5 unravelled strands.

Cyber Flirt

Who has time to date in person anymore?
Next time you hop online for a bit of inter-flirting,
wrap your toes in cabled splendor.

by MARY McCALL

SKILL LEVEL
Experienced

FINISHED MEASUREMENTS
Foot circumference 8½"/21.5cm

Leg length 8½"/21.5cm

Foot length 9"/23cm

MATERIALS AND TOOLS
Approx total: 440 yd/396m of ③ worsted weight yarn, superwash wool, in gray

Knitting needles: 3.25mm (size 3 U.S.) set of 4 double-pointed needles *or size to obtain gauge*

Stitch markers

Cable needle

Stitch holder

Waste yarn

Yarn needle

GAUGE
26 sts and 32 rows = 4"/10cm in Stockinette Stitch (knit every round)

Always take time to check your gauge.

Special Abbreviations
Dry Bones Cable (DBC): Slip 4 sts to cable needle and hold in front, drop the next st off the left needle, slip the 3 purl sts back onto the left needle, slip the dropped knit st back onto left needle, k1, p3 from left needle, k1 tbl from cable needle.

C8B (Cable 8 Back): Slip 4 sts onto cable needle and hold in back, k2, k2 from cable needle and bring to front, k2, k2 from cable needle.

TOE
Cast on 20 stitches with waste yarn. Taking care not to twist stitches, join to work in the round.

Knit 1 round. With the "real" yarn, leave a nice long tail and knit the next round. Distribute the stitches as follows: 5 stitches each on needles #1 and #3, and 10 stitches on needle #2.

Toe Increases
Round 1 (Increase):

Needle #1: Knit to last 2 sts, kfb, k1.

Needle #2: K1, kfb, knit to last 2 sts, kfb, k1.

Needle #3: K1, kfb, knit to end.

Round 2: Knit.

Repeat rounds 1 and 2, until there are 56 sts.

INSTEP
Redistribute stitches as follows: 14 sts on needle #1 (for first half of sole), 28 sts on needle #2 (for instep), 14 sts on needle #3 (for second half of sole). The beginning of each round is at the center of the sole.

Round 1:

Needle #1: Knit;

Needle #2: Work row 1 of Instep Chart;

Needle #3: Knit.

Round 2:

Needle #1: Knit;

Needle #2: Work next row of Instep Chart;

Needle #3: Knit.

Repeat round 2 until all 40 rows of the Instep Chart are completed, or until foot measures 2"/5cm less than desired foot length. Note: If you need more than the 40 rows of the Instep Chart, continue over the center 28 sts of the Leg Chart. Take note of where you stop (on Instep or Leg Chart). Take care to begin in the same place when beginning the leg of the sock.

SHORT ROW HEEL

Note: The heel is worked in short rows. A short-row heel is the heel that most resembles the heel of a commercial sock. It is worked on half of the leg stitches (28 in this case).

Place the 28 instep stitches on a holder. Work back and forth on heel sts only. Place a marker at the center of the heel stitches. You will be leaving the last stitch (or the last unwrapped stitch) unworked on each row. This is the stitch that gets wrapped.

Row 1 (RS): Knit to last st, w&t.

Row 2: Purl to last st, w&t.

Row 3: Knit to 1 st before wrapped st, w&t.

Row 4: Purl to 1 st before wrapped st, w&t.

Repeat rows 3 and 4 until you have 1"/2.5cm of unwrapped stitches at the center of the heel (½"/1.5cm on either side of the marker); end with a WS row.

Next row: Knit to first wrapped st, pick up the wrap and place it on the left needle, knit the stitch and wrap together, turn.

Next row: Purl to first wrapped st, pick up the wrap and place it on the left needle, purl the stitch and wrap together, turn.

Repeat the last 2 rows until all wrapped stitches have been worked. End ready to work from center of heel (needle #1).

LEG

When working the first round, pick up a stitch or two where the heel meets the instep stitches. Decrease them away on the next round (or two) with k2tog. This will help prevent the hole that sometimes forms there.

Note: Take care to start the leg pattern where you left off when working the instep pattern.

Working from Leg Chart (or Instep Chart then Leg Chart, if you worked a shorter foot) until all rounds of Leg Chart have been completed or leg measures 2"/5cm less than desired length.

Ribbing

Round 1 (decrease): P1, k2tog, p2, k2tog, k1, p2, k2tog, k1, p2, k2, p3, k2, p2, k2tog, k1, p2, k2tog, k1, p2, k2, p3, k2, p2, k2tog, k1, p2, k2tog, k1, p2, k2tog, p1—48 sts.

Round 2: P1, k1, (p2, k2) 3 times, p3, (k2, p2) 3 times, k2, p3, (k2, p2) 3 times, k1, p1.

Repeat round 2 until ribbing measures 2"/5cm or desired length of ribbing.

FINISHING

Bind off using a stretchy bind off.

Finish Toe

Remove the waste yarn and put the "real" stitches back onto two double-pointed needles, being sure that the toe is oriented correctly. Use Kitchener Stitch to sew the two sets of stitches together.

Weave in ends.

This project was knit with:

Cascade Yarn's Cascade 220, worsted weight, 100% superwash wool, 3.5oz/100g = approx 220yd/198m per skein
2 skeins, color #900

Many thanks to Robley Brown (now deceased) for showing me that a short-row heel can fit, and for giving me permission to paraphrase her heel instructions.

18%
of sock knitters admit to looking at online socks more than three times a day.

leg chart

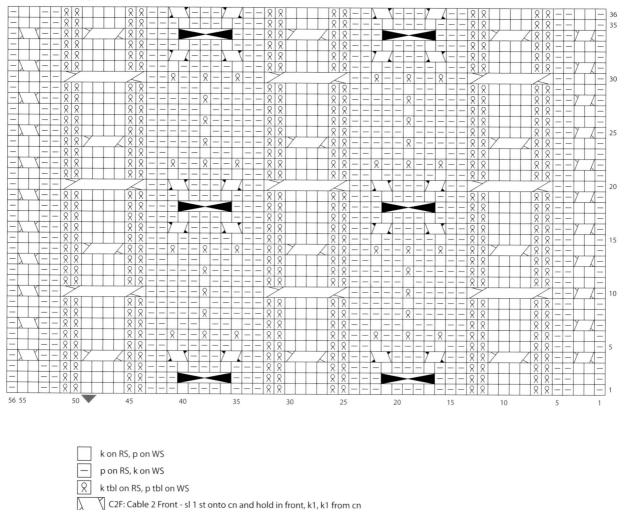

k on RS, p on WS

p on RS, k on WS

k tbl on RS, p tbl on WS

C2F: Cable 2 Front - sl 1 st onto cn and hold in front, k1, k1 from cn

C2B: Cable 2 Back - sl 1 st onto cn and hold in back, k1, k1 from cn

C2Fp tbl: Cable 2 Front purl - sl 1 st onto cn and hold in front, p1, k1 tbl from cn

C2Bp tbl: Cable 2 Back purl - sl 1 st onto cn and hold in back, k1 tbl, p1 from cn

C4B: Cable 4 Back - sl 2 sts onto cn and hold in back, k2, k2 from cn

C8B (Cable 8 Back): Slip 4 stitches onto cn and hold in back, k2, k2 from cn and bring to front, k2, k2 from cn

Dry Bones Cable (DBC): Slip 4 sts to cn and hold in front, drop the next st off the left needle, slip the 3 purl sts back onto the left needle, slip the dropped knit st back onto left needle, k1, p3 from left needle, k1 tbl from cn

instep chart

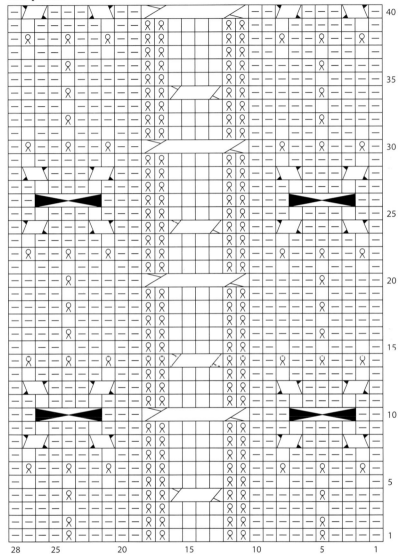

Zhen Zen

A Sunday afternoon nap, sipping chai tea, listening to Yo-Yo Ma, lounging in your handknit socks…take time to relish serene moments.

by HEIDI SCHEPPMANN

TOE

Using Turkish cast on, cast on 11 (13, 15) sts on each of two circular needles. Work each needle as follows: K2, p7 (9, 11), k2.

Round 1: (K2, MPR, purl to last 2 sts of needle, MPL, k2) twice—13 (15, 17) sts on each needle.

Round 2: (K2, purl to last 2 sts of needle, k2) twice.

Repeat last 2 rounds 9 (10, 11) more times—31 (35, 39) sts on each needle.

FOOT

Set up: Slip the first two and last two stitches of needle #2 onto needle #1. Note: Needle #1 holds the instep stitches and needle #2 holds the sole stitches.

Round 1:

Needle #1: Sl 2, k2, p to last 4 sts, k4—35 (39, 43) sts;

Needle #2: Purl—27 (31, 35) sts.

Round 2:

Needle #1: Work chart A (Scotch Faggoting), p2 (4, 6), work chart B (Ogee Lace), p2 (4, 6), work chart A;

Needle #2: Purl.

Repeat last round until sock measures 3 (3¼, 3½)"/7.5 (8.5, 9)cm shorter than desired foot length.

Note: This measurement is dependent on a row gauge of 13 rows per inch. If your row gauge varies, divide 32 (36, 40) by row gauge and round up to the nearest ½"/1.5cm to determine the length of the heel. Work foot until sock measures same as your heel measurement less the foot length.

SKILL LEVEL
Experienced

FINISHED MEASUREMENTS
Foot circumference 7 (8, 8½)"/18 (20.5, 21.5)cm

Leg length 7"/18cm (or custom)

Foot length custom

MATERIALS AND TOOLS
Approx total: 438yd/394m of (1) fingering weight yarn, merino/polyamide/silk blend, in beige

Knitting needles: 2mm (size 0 U.S.) set of 2 circular needles 16–24"/40.5–61cm, *or size to obtain gauge*

Stitch markers

Yarn needle

GAUGE
36 sts and 52 rows = 4"/10cm in Stockinette Stitch (knit every round)

Always take time to check your gauge.

Special Abbreviations

PU & K (used only on knit side of work): Sl1 knitwise. Pick up wrap and slip up and over slipped stitch. Insert left needle through fronts of stitch and wrap, work as ssk.

Final PU & K of row: Sl1 knitwise. Pick up wrap and slip up and over slipped stitch. Sl1 knitwise. Insert left needle through fronts of two stitches and wrap, work as sssk.

PU & P (used on purl side of work): Pick up wrap around first stitch on left needle. Slip up and over stitch. Purl the stitch and its wrap together (P2tog).

Final PU & P of row: Pick up wrap around first stitch on left needle. Slip up and over stitch. Purl the stitch, its wrap, and the next stitch together (P3tog).

MPR: With left needle, pick up strand between needles from back to front. Purl into the front of this strand.

MPL: With left needle, pick up strand between needles from front to back. Purl into the back of this strand.

Shape Gusset
Round 1:

Needle #1: Work in pattern as established;

Needle #2: MPR, purl to end, MPL.

Round 2:

Needle #1: Work in pattern as established;

Needle #2: Purl.

Repeat rounds 1 and 2 until there are 94 (106, 118) stitches: (35 [39, 43] sts on needle #1, 59 [67, 75] sts on needle #2).

Take note of which chart pattern round you have just worked. You will need to resume on the next chart round after the heel.

Turn Heel
Note: The heel will be worked back and forth on needle #2 only.

Row 1 (RS): Turn work, sl 1, k41 (47, 53), w&t.

Row 2: P25 (29, 33), w&t.

Row 3: K to 1 st before wrapped st, w&t.

Row 4: P to 1 st before wrapped st, w&t.

Repeat last 2 rows 7 (8, 10) more times (for 18 [20, 24] rows total). There will be 9 (10, 12) stitches wrapped on each end of needle.

Pick-Up Wraps
Row 1: Sl 1, k to first wrapped st, PU & K 8 (9, 11) sts; pick up the next wrap and sssk the st, its wrap, and the next st, turn.

Row 2: Sl 1, p to first wrapped st, PU & P 8 (9, 11) sts; pick up the next wrap and p3tog the st, its wrap, and the next st, turn.

Heel Flap
Continue to work back and forth on heel stitches for the heel flap.

Row 1 (RS): Sl 1, k25 (29, 33), p2tog, turn.

Row 2: Sl 1, p25 (29, 33), ssk, turn.

Repeat last 2 rows until all stitches have been worked (30 [34, 38] rows total). You will have 27 (31, 35) stitches, consisting of 25 (29, 33) purl stitches, with one knit stitch on each end.

LEG
Resume working in the round.

Round 1:

Needle #1: Work chart A, p 2 (4, 6), work chart B, p 2 (4, 6), work chart A;

Needle #2: Purl.

Repeat last round until you have completed round 22 of chart B.

Next round:

Needle #1: Work chart A, p2 (4, 6), work chart B, p2 (4, 6), work chart A;

Needle #2: P2 (4, 6), work chart B from the beginning, p 2 (4, 6).

Repeat last round until leg measures ½"/1.5cm less than desired leg length, completing the final 6 rounds of the chart to finish.

Hem

Round 1: Knit.

Rounds 2–7: Purl.

Round 8: *K2tog, yo; repeat from * around.

Rounds 9–14: Knit.

FINISHING

Cut yarn, leaving a tail five times longer than the foot circumference. Thread the tail onto a yarn needle. Fold hem at round 8 (the yarn overs will create a natural folding point). Whipstitch each stitch from needle to the back of the knit stitches of round 1. Weave in ends.

This project was knit with:

Regia's Silk, fingering weight, 55% Merino wool, 25% polyamide, 20% silk, 1.75oz/50g = approx 219yd/197m per skein 2 skeins, color #005

chart a (scotch faggoting)

chart b (ogee lace)

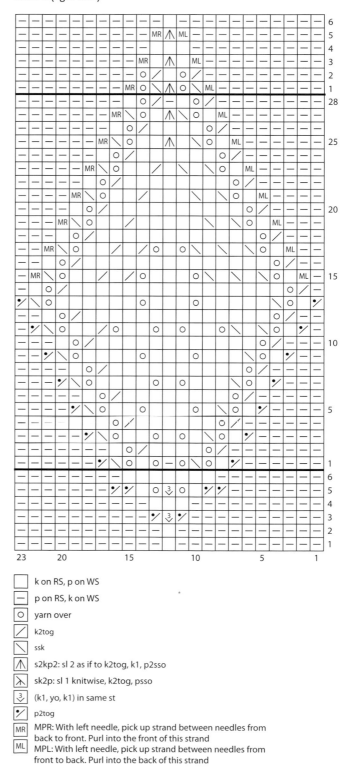

k on RS, p on WS

— p on RS, k on WS

O yarn over

/ k2tog

\ ssk

/\ s2kp2: sl 2 as if to k2tog, k1, p2sso

sk2p: sl 1 knitwise, k2tog, psso

(k1, yo, k1) in same st

p2tog

MR MPR: With left needle, pick up strand between needles from back to front. Purl into the front of this strand

ML MPL: With left needle, pick up strand between needles from front to back. Purl into the back of this strand

173

About the Designers

Kathryn Alexander is an internationally known textile artist—a spinner, weaver, dyer, and knitter—whose work is characterized by an abundance of color, richly textured surfaces, and whimsical designs. Her work has been featured in several magazines, including *Fiberarts*, *Surface Design*, *Ornament*, *Spin Off*, and *Knits*, and in a number of books, including *Knitting in America*, *Fiberarts Design Book 7*, *Memory on Cloth*, *Design!*, and *Knitting Memories*.

Dr. Laura Andersson is one of those folks who doesn't know how to retire. For over 26 years, she took part in nationally funded biophysical research into human health and taught at both Ivy League and Midwestern institutions. Now, she is happily continuing to play with light and color via knitwear design. She has recently edited and published two *Friendly Socks* collections, now on CD. To see more of her work, visit her online at www.siriusknitting.com.

Star Athena is a spinner, knitter, and lover of all things fiber. She has contributed articles and patterns to a number of places—print and online—including Knitscene, knitty.com, and Ravelry. Star was a guest on DIY's "Knitty Gritty" and started the annual online spin-along, The Tour de Fleece, to spin yarn along with the Tour de France. Her adventures in knitting and spinning can be found in her blog keeponknittinginthefreeworld.blogspot.com.

Kate Atherley is a knitwear designer and teacher based in Toronto. She enjoys creating intriguing new variations on old favorites and believes that socks can be just as fun and personal as any other item worn next to the skin. You can follow her progress at www.wisehildaknits.com.

Kate Blackburn learned to knit socks three years ago and has been obsessed ever since. She is co-editor of The Inside Loop (www.theinsideloop.com), an online magazine dedicated to promoting fiber arts in the United Kingdom.

Knitwear designer and author-**Cathy Carron** left behind a corporate career in marketing once her daughters Emma and Lydia were born. Ever since, her focus has been on hand knitting, first as a small business owner and importer of children's sweaters, next as a writer and researcher on "hand knitting for the military during wartime." Most recently, Cathy has authored two books on hand-knitting technique—*Hip Knit Hats* (Lark, 2005) and *Knitting Sweaters from the Top Down* (Lark, 2007). You can see more of Cathy's work at www.pondedge.net.

Sauniell Nicole Connally, once a software engineer, is now pursuing her passion for fashion design full time in New York City. She has been in knitwear design for over seven years and creates for magazine and book publications as well her own site: saunshine.blogspot.com.

Maia Discoe learned to knit, sew, and cook as a young girl from her mother and grandmother, eventually trading in her sewing machine for circular and double-pointed needles. A self-taught designer, she lives in Richmond, California, with her wonderful husband, Roger, her fabulous daughter, Kay, and her charming dog, Sammie. Maia co-owns Tactile, a fiber arts studio where she dyes yarns and spinning fiber with organic, sustainable, and fair-trade natural dyes.

Adrienne Fong, aka Lotus Blossom, didn't initially understand all the fuss about hand-knit socks. After knitting her first pair of socks about five years ago, she "got" it and has since been working on her sock yarn collection. She has designed socks for The Knitter, Blue Moon Fiber Arts, Crystal Palace Yarns, P.T. Yarns, SWTC, and Robyn's Nest. Adrienne blogs at bellybuttonknits.blogspot.com and can be found on Ravelry as bellybuttonknits. Adrienne sends special thanks to Barbara Mellert for test knitting.

Melanie Gibbons knits and spins in Northern Virginia with her very supportive husband, son, dog, and cat. She designed and hosted the Original Mystery Stole Knit Along, as well as Mystery Stoles 2 and 3. Melanie blogs about her knitting and spinning adventures at pinklemontwist.blogspot.com or can be found on Ravelry as PinkLemon.

Sivia Harding is a designer who dabbles in lace, beads, and, most recently, socks. She has been self-publishing her knitting patterns for several years, and her work can be seen in the online magazine Knitty, the print magazine *Yarn*, and the books *Knitgrrl 2*, *Big Girl Knits*, *More Big Girl Knits*, and *No Sheep for You*. Her patterns are for sale at numerous yarn stores and on www.siviaharding.com.

Lynn Hershberger has focused on bright colors all her life, and she surrounds herself with color in all possible ways. Whether it's painting the porch purple, painting stars on her car, creating with polymer clay, printmaking, mail art, felt-making, costuming, knitting or dyeing wool yarns, colors are always playing an important part in Lynn's life. Visit LynnH's SockTour, her ColorJoy blog, and other delights at www.colorjoy.com.

Gina House, aka SleepyEyes, is a mother to two boys and loves to knit, spin yarn, design, and read Tarot. Her designs have been featured on OnePlanetYarnAndFiber.com, Ravelry.com, YarnAndFiber.com, and on her blog, SleepyEyesKnitting.blogspot.com. The Amanda Hat, Christmas Eve Cabled Mitts, and Lisha Lace Scarf are her most popular patterns and also her favorites. Her fun and quirky podcast, Sleepy Eyes Knits, is available on iTunes.

Alyson Johnson, aka the Yo-Yo, is a knitter, spinner, designer, and dyer who lives in Florida with a baffled but supportive husband. They have an indeterminate amount of dogs and cats, and when not working a day job, she blogs at terribleknitknit.blogspot.com and runs The YoYo Yarn Shop at theyoyo.etsy.com.

Kirsten Kapur has been sewing, knitting, painting, and drawing for as long as she can remember. For many years she worked in the garment industry as a textile and apparel designer before retiring to raise her family. She now draws on her past experiences as she designs knitting patterns from her home in the rolling hills of northwestern New Jersey. Kirsten can be found online at throughtheloops.typepad.com.

Designing is a natural activity for **Ann Kingstone** who is happiest when expending creative energy. She is currently living in a noisy Yorkshire mill-town with her "exuberant" family and believes that utopia would be a home in open country with sheep, goats, her spinning and knitting tools, and a massive workroom! A love of traditional patterns inspires much of Ann's work, which can be found at her blog spinninginstead.blogspot.com or on Ravelry as spinningmaid.

Susan Pierce Lawrence is an ocean-loving Bostonian, transplanted to the landlocked state of Utah. She learned to knit as a child but rediscovered the craft during her last year of law school. Susan has a well-documented weakness for sock yarn and chronicles her obsession with knitting and her relentless efforts to spin up her fiber stash on her blog knittingasfastasican.com.

Janine Le Cras lives, works, and windsurfs the beautiful island of Guernsey, located midway between the United Kingdom and France. She learned to knit at the knee of her grandmother and has always loved the history of the craft as practiced on the island. It is said that Queen Elizabeth I wore stockings knitted on Guernsey, so Janine is carrying on the tradition, spreading the word, one sock at a time.

Mary McCall has been designing knitting patterns for over 10 years, prompted by the fact that her handspun yarn refused to conform to commercial gauge. A drafter by day, she dreams up new patterns by night. She can be found on the web at www.wool-fiber-originals.com; on her blog at catmccall.blogspot.com; or on Ravelry as catmccall.

Jolene Mosley has been knitting for years and designing as she goes—keeping herself busy and happy. She enjoys life's journeys at the knit shop or at home with her husband, two daughters, and one son.

Born and raised in Seattle, **Mary Jane Mucklestone** has always had a fascination with textiles. After receiving her BFA in Printmaking from Pratt Institute, she was lured into the New York City garment industry working for indy and haute couture designers. After moving to Maine to start a family, she decided knitting was a convenient and non-toxic outlet for creativity in her new life with small children underfoot. Currently she designs from home and teaches a few workshops each year.

Karen Neal self-publishes individual patterns for hand knitters under the business name Karendipity: Serendipitous Designs. As a knitting instructor for The Studio Knitting and Needlepoint in Kansas City, Missouri, she was encouraged by her fellow knitters to share her original designs. The success of her first pattern, Hand Painted Gloves, encouraged her to enter the world of hand-knit designs.

Lindsay Obermeyer exhibits her art in galleries and museums around the world, including the Museum of Art and Design in New York and the Boston Museum of Fine Arts. She lives in Chicago with her daughter and two dogs, and when she's not working in the studio or teaching workshops, she can be found puttering in her garden. To see more of Lindsay's art, check out her website at www.lbostudio.com.

Mona Schmidt lives in Montreal and loves designing socks. She has been published in *Interweave Knits*, *Knitscene*, and *Lace Style*. Her "Embossed Leaves Socks" from *Knits* Winter 2005 can be found in *Favorite Socks* and have been knit all over the world. Mona works for JCA, Inc., designing knitwear for all ages.

Amy Polcyn has been designing since 2005, and her work has appeared in *Knitter's*, *Cast On*, *Creative Knitting*, *Knit N' Style*, *Knit Simple*, and several books. Additionally, she has designed extensively for SWTC, Nashua Handknits, Shibui Knits, Aslan Trends, and numerous other yarn companies. Previously an elementary school teacher, Amy now works full-time as a designer and technical editor. She blogs about all things knitting at frottez.blogspot.com.

SaRi knits and designs from her home in Berlin, Germany. After more than 25 years of passionate entanglement with yarn and two pointy sticks, she has achieved a broad background in both traditional and modern knitting techniques. She records her knitting on her blog sarismindfulknitting.blogspot.com. More of her designs can be found in online knitting magazines and in yarn shops under the pattern line SaRi.

Heidi Scheppmann started knitting five years ago, and hasn't put down the needles since. She splits time between her New York City apartment and her cabin in upstate New York. Heidi can usually be found knitting in her apartment, her cabin in the woods, in the car, on the subway, on airplanes—basically anywhere she can take her needles. You can read about her knitting life at yarnmule.blogspot.com.

Pauline Schultz, a TKGA Master Knitter in both hand and machine, has been knitting since before the flood. She seems fated to live in states that have little need of knits like Hawaii and currently Arizona, but that doesn't stop the needles. Lace is her favorite, but any yarn or project that turns her on starts the needles.

Index